POLICY STUDIES IN EMPLOYMENT AND WELFARE NUMBER 21

General Editor: Sar A. Levitan

Work and Welfare in New York City

Miriam Ostow and
Anna B. Dutka

Foreword by Eli Ginzberg

The Johns Hopkins University Press, Baltimore and London

This report was prepared for the Manpower Administration, U.S. Department of Labor, under research contract 21-36-73-51, authorized by Title I of the Manpower Development and Training Act. Since contractors performing research under government sponsorship are encouraged to express their own judgment freely, the report does not necessarily represent the Department's official opinion or policy. Moreover, the contractor is solely responsible for the factual accuracy of all material developed in the report.

Reproduction in whole or in part permitted for any purpose of the U.S. government.

Manufactured in the United States of America

The Johns Hopkins University Press, Baltimore, Maryland 21218
The Johns Hopkins University Press Ltd., London

Library of Congress Catalog Card Number 75-11357
ISBN 0-8018-1735-8 (cloth)
ISBN 0-8018-1736-6 (paper)

Library of Congress Cataloging in Publication data will be found on the last printed page of this book.

Contents

Tables

Acknowledgments

Research is by nature a collaborative enterprise requiring a multiplicity of inputs and skills. The present study of work and welfare in New York City represents the merger of two major concerns of Professor Eli Ginzberg, founder and director of the Conservation of Human Resources Project: the social and economic waste of human resources caused by long-term unemployment and the operation of present-day metropolitan labor markets. It was his perception that the debate over social welfare policy might be illuminated by an analysis focusing upon these issues. Freedom to pursue the inquiry as we judged best, combined with his incisive review of progress at successive phases, constituted a most salubrious working climate, for which we are grateful.

Our research would not have been possible had not Jules Sugarman, former administrator of New York City's Human Resources Administration, shared our concern with the issues it addresses and offered us access to the resources of the Department of Social Services. Among its members who were particularly helpful were Herbert Rosenbloom, of the Administrator's office; Arthur Schiff, Stephen Leeds, and Erla Alexander, of the Office of Policy Research; and Elizabeth Lubetkin. Actual collaborators were the numerous anonymous staff members within the welfare centers who searched 2,000 case records and completed the lengthy and detailed questionnaires which are the subject of this investigation. We wish we could thank each of them individually; instead, we can only convey a collective acknowledgment through the person of

Mr. Edward H. Corn, then assistant to the director of the Bureau of Public Assistance, who served efficiently and good-humoredly as expediter and coordinator of our extensive data-gathering activity within the Department.

Dr. Blanche Bernstein, Director of Research, Center for New York City Affairs, the New School for Social Research, was an extremely generous consultant from initial conceptualization to critical reading of the final draft.

Not the least of the fringe benefits of association with the Conservation of Human Resources Project is the opportunity to draw on the special competences of its interdisciplinary staff. Among our benefactors have been Dr. Marcia Freedman, Dr. Beatrice Reubens, and Gretchen Maclachlan. Alice Yohalem's reading helped us to clarify our exposition at many points. Our heaviest debt is to Dr. Charles Brecher, who has been our coauthor in fact if not in name all along the way.

We hope that the final work justifies the efforts of our collaborators, but in any case errors of fact, analysis, and interpretation are exclusively our own.

Foreword by Eli Ginzberg

There are issues that engage the public that consistently generate more heat than light. One such issue is the attitude of the citizenry toward people on public welfare. After five or more years of blistering depression, in the mid-1930s, the *New York Times* editorialized about the unwillingness of the unemployed to go out and find jobs for themselves—this when the unemployment rate was hovering around the 20 percent mark! Similar questions based on similar assumptions surfaced again in the latter 1960s, when the American economy was in the midst of what turned out to be the most sustained boom in its history.

It is more than a hundred and fifty years since the founders of political economy in Great Britain, particularly Robert Malthus and David Ricardo, warned that if people without work and income could, for the asking, receive relief, the country faced a great and present danger: the rolls would swell to a point where the savings of frugal citizens would be taxed away to provide the revenue that government had to raise to cover the mounting costs of the Poor Laws. Unless the rising numbers on the rolls could be checked and reduced, the founders of political economy saw only trouble ahead: transfer payments from the provident to the improvident would prevent the accumulation of capital and would undermine the growth of the British economy. Hence they advocated that the granting of relief be subjected to tightened regulations so that those who could work and support themselves and their dependents would be encouraged to do so rather than to look to government for their sustenance. The passage in 1970 of the Talmadge Amendment to the Social Security Act reflected the same concerns and looked to similar remedies. There is a deep strain, at least in the American tradition, that the physically able should look to their own labor as the source of their support, the only possible exception being female heads of households with young children, who, it was presumed, at least at the time of the passage of the Social Security Act in 1935, should be assisted to remain at home to care for them. To this date many states provide no general assistance for the able-bodied person who is without work and income.

The present study was designed toward the end of the economic expansion of the 1960s, when jobs were relatively plentiful but the urban relief rolls were expanding—some would say exploding— particularly with respect to those who presumptively were not physically incapacitated to hold a job, whatever other handicaps might interfere with their employability. Since the authors have described the many steps from research design to research conclusions, I will select for comment a few themes that surfaced during the course of this investigation that warrant attention, even though they may not, at first inspection, appear to be central for either research or policy. These themes relate to the difficulties of designing and carrying out an investigation that require the cooperation of a bureaucracy, be it public or private; the limitations of using existing administrative data for analytical and policy assessments; the confusions that flow from the tendency of scholars and politicians alike to treat individuals with quite disparate characteristics as if they belonged to the same group; and a failure to fashion remedial action for the individual, preference being shown for providing the same services to all eligibles.

It has long been recognized by those who are interested in such matters that a principal drawback in all social science inquiry is the unwillingness of individuals in control of significant data to provide the outsider access to them for fear that they individually, the organization whose interests they are paid to protect, or the values that they hold dear may be jeopardized by the results of the inquiry. The risks and dangers of affording outsiders access to basic information are present and often overwhelming; the gains, if any, are putative, long-range, and diffuse. If one can say no, why should a responsible corporate officer or government official say yes to a request for assistance, especially if the investigator is seeking to explore important, not peripheral, issues? Admittedly, the citizen's right to public records stands on a different footing from his request for corporate data, but these differences should not be exaggerated. The government official has the responsibility to protect the confidentiality of client records, and he must be concerned with the political exploitation of unfavorable information.

The proposal for the present study by the Conservation of Human Resources Project received the prompt approval of the Human Resources Administration, whose research department expressed interest in the issues and questions to be explored. Nevertheless, the actual investigation was obstructed for many months, a victim of the increasing public debate concerning the system nationally and specifically the local department and the resistance of the latter to any further scrutiny of its records. The nonpolitical nature of the inquiry and the willingness to share findings with the department prior to publication were initially insufficient to overcome objections to external research. Only the senior investigator's ability to absorb frustration, her willingness to deal objectively with the myriad reservations that emerged, and her determination to convince the officialdom of the intrinsic merit of the study enabled it to proceed. Once underway, however, the present study became in every sense a cooperative undertaking between the Conservation of Human Resources Project, Columbia University, and the Human Resources Administration, New York City. Without the wholehearted interest of the administrator, Jules Sugarman, the unflagging assistance of the departmental coordinator who was assigned to the project, and the efforts of supervisors and staff in practically all of the income maintenance centers this study never could have been carried out.

Every organization develops the data it needs to meet urgent organizational demands, and little more. Basic data collection is time-consuming and costly, and often the decisionmakers do not perceive it to be useful. Where money transactions are the key to client services, as in the case of welfare payments to eligible applicants, a bureaucracy's concerns are, first, to see that only those who meet the legal and administrative criteria are accepted on the rolls and, second, to see that they receive no more than that to which they are entitled. In short, the recordkeeping is geared to financial accountability. Legislators and administrators are concerned with the total cost of welfare.

It is possible to use administrative recordkeeping to tease out selective information about the characteristics of those who receive welfare and to use these to illuminate alternative policies, as Ostow and Dutka have done, but the fact remains that the available data were gathered and processed in the first instance for other purposes. Accordingly, we know much less than we need to know about the interface of work and welfare. Surely no records were ever collected either in New York City or anywhere else, to speak specifically to that issue. What the present monograph succeeds in doing is to illuminate the work-welfare theme from administrative records designed to answer other questions.

If the public and the politician are seriously concerned about the high costs of the welfare system and suspect that the system harbors a large number of persons who should be forced to support themselves, relevant data must be collected and analyzed. Considering that welfare payments run to more than $12 billion annually, including $4 billion for assistance to the aged and the disabled, and that these large expenditures have been viewed with suspicion and animosity by a large number of taxpayers and legislators, it is difficult to understand why we still balk at making the effort necessary to ascertain the facts. Apparently, there are political forces that keep us mired in our present uncertainty and confusion rather than permit us to learn what the truth is or at least to come closer to it.

In late 1974, the newspapers carried reports that the federal administration was considering a new legislative approach to reform of the welfare system. Its aim would be to replace major in-kind programs for the poor and the near poor, such as medical assistance, food stamps, and public housing, with a comprehensive cash grant. This is an expanded version of earlier Nixon proposals based on the application of the negative income tax. Reference is made to the proposed legislation to stress the heterogeneous composition of the welfare population and the desirability of designing public policies that are responsive to the diversity of the recipients and the changing nature of the economy that determines their prospects for future employment.

With respect to the heterogeneity of the welfare population, Ostow and Dutka, who oversampled with an eye to enlarging the pool of employables, make the following distinctions: the relatively low-skilled working man who holds down a regular job but who is on welfare because his earnings fail to cover the minimum needs of his large family, which usually has in excess of four children; men and women with a recurrent pattern of employment who appear to be vulnerable to a cyclical softening of the labor market; and workers whose intermittent employment seems to be more closely linked to personal difficulties, primarily health, which force them to give up their jobs at least for a time. Then there are a large number of women with little or no work experience who have been on welfare for many years and who, even though they have no young children at home, make little or no effort to find a regular job (although some of them may be supplementing their relief checks by part-time earnings). Finally, there are the young people coming of working age, many with indifferent educational and vocational preparation, who experience various orders of difficulty in linking into the job market, especially in periods of substantial unemployment.

Recapitulating, we find:

1) the regularly employed with earnings below welfare standards;
2) the intermittently employed who lose their jobs in periods of slack employment;
3) those who go on welfare because a health problem or other defect prevents them from continuing to work, at least for a time;
4) the large number of female heads of households who appear to have made a quasi-permanent adjustment to the welfare rolls; and
5) the adolescents supported by welfare who have not yet made a successful transition into the world of work.

One need do no more than inspect the foregoing to realize that any attempt to treat the welfare population as an undifferentiated group of unemployables or employables is clearly erroneous. There is no more basis in Ostow and Dutka's study for supporting Joseph Califano's statement, when he served in the late 1960s as President Johnson's aide, to the effect that there were practically no employables on the welfare rolls than there is for the frequently expressed Congressional belief that the welfare rolls contain a high proportion of employables who prefer welfare to work. Both positions suffer from the same error of seeing the welfare population as a homogeneous group inviting the same type of social intervention. If the present study does nothing else, it stands as a warning against specious oversimplifications. Once one recognizes that the welfare rolls are populated by a significant number of subgroups that must be differentiated if they are to be assisted to make a more effective economic and social adjustment, it follows that public policy must be sensitive to the major problems that each confronts. A single policy cannot be responsive to such diversified needs. A few suggestions may help to clarify the critical relation between improved diagnosis and more effective therapy.

The first group of regularly employed, low-income earners need income supplementation, which is what welfare now provides them in New York City, though not in many other parts of the country. The proponents of welfare reform are correct in recognizing that something should be done to help the "working poor." The question that remains moot is whether the negative-income-tax approach is the preferred answer in the face of the wide geographic variations in earnings, cost of living, community outlook, and other conditions.

To the extent that health or other personal characteristics explain why a person is forced out of employment or is hindered from getting back into employment, it is highly questionable that the answer lies solely in nationally uniform monetary benefits. What such a person (or family) requires is improved access to improved services. Admittedly, such linkages are not easy to establish and maintain, but it behooves the welfare reformer to recognize that revising the welfare system alone will not assure many of the outcomes that such reform seeks. Clearly this observation holds as well for the adolescent and young adult who are encountering serious difficulties in linking into the world of work. The transition from school to work necessitates new ties among the educational authorities, the employment service, training institutions, employers, trade unions, counselors, and still other institutions and mechanisms that potentially can help to reduce the serious slippage that now exists. Nor does it make sense to consider all women on AFDC as a homogeneous group. Some are young, relatively well-schooled, with but one dependent child. Others are over fifty, poorly educated and in poor health, and have had no work experience in 20 years. Public policy that fails to be responsive to this striking differences among these two subgroups is doomed from the outset to frustration. Undoubtedly, legislators and administrators seek generic answers to complex social problems, but in the face of such incontrovertible differences among people the same policy is certain to fail some, and if it seeks a middle ground, it will fail many.

There runs deep in the American experience the belief that people who find themselves on welfare lack some basic personal strengths, above all the desire to work and to be independent. It would be overdefensive to say that there may not be many thousands of such people on the welfare rolls, but it would be a wild leap into the unknown to fit the millions who are on welfare into this category. When national unemployment is 5–6 percent, the rates for minority group members tend to run to 10–12 percent, and considerably higher in certain cities. In brief, shortfalls in available jobs, particularly jobs that hold some promise of continuity even if they pay only little more than the minimum wage, are characteristic of many urban economies with large numbers on the welfare rolls.

If the American people really believe that individuals capable of working should be forced to work for their daily bread, the issue of job availability must be faced. It has been one of the two missing ingredients of all recent discussions of welfare reform.

The other issue also not adequately considered in recent welfare reform is how far the public is willing to go to alter the philosophy underlying the original commitment to help provide for heads of households to rear their children. If the public now believes that, rather than stay at home and care for their own children, mothers should be encouraged or forced to accept paid employment, then the same public must provide more by way of childcare facilities.

Unless it can overcome its continuing ambivalence on this issue, there is little prospect for any significant reform of AFDC. There is nothing easy or inexpensive about reforming AFDC to provide even young women with acceptable childcare facilities while pressuring them to seek training and work. But unless the issue is tackled seriously, no significant changes can be anticipated.

Nevertheless, a solution of the childcare problem is a necessary but not sufficient condition for true reform of AFDC. Only a minority of the present caseload would be able to earn enough to cover the additional work-related expenditures and have an income above the prevailing welfare standard. Hence, many would continue to require income supplementation. It might make good sense, as Ostow and Dutka suggest, to absorb these two costly and difficult adjustments if one puts a high premium on preventing the long-term accommodation of young women to welfare. But if the public opts for meaningful reform of AFDC, it must understand what that reform is about.

A careful reading of this monograph illuminates a great many aspects of the work-welfare interface, only a few of which have been noted above. What their painstaking study reveals, above all else, is the need for more incisive analysis of these complex relationships before new policies are enacted; the warning that no singular change, even one so radical as the replacement of all welfare programs with a comprehensive negative income tax, would prove responsive to the range of problems that face the welfare population; and that the true reform of welfare implies a reform of work which the United States must belatedly face up to by implementing the Employment Act of 1946.

Work and
Welfare in
New York City

1

The Issues

Employment and employability first became a major issue in public assistance policy more than a decade ago. It gained importance with the development of federal antipoverty efforts in the mid-sixties and today dominates thinking about welfare and welfare reform. This emphasis represents a distinct modification of the original goal of the American Social Security System. When the Social Security Law was enacted in 1935, in the aftermath of the Great Depression, it was designed to provide income to alleviate the abject poverty of specific groups of the population who were excluded from the labor force and whom it was considered socially desirable to free from the necessity of seeking a livelihood. How did such a major conceptual change come about?

Throughout the sixties, mounting costs of public assistance, shifting socioeconomic profiles of metropolitan populations, structural alterations in the labor market, changing perceptions of the social and economic rights of individuals, and the quickened pace of the civil rights movement all converged to make ongoing income maintenance for the working-age population the subject of passionate criticism from right, left, and center. Public assistance became one of the most politically embattled domestic issues of the decade. The paradoxical expansion of income transfers in dollar volume and number of recipients during a period of affluence constituted a fiscal and political threat to municipalities and states, a major irritant to taxpayers, and a dilemma to legislators confronted with the need to reestablish control over a program whose original aims seemed to have been transformed and whose consequences clearly ran counter to expectations. Stated another way, during a period of full employment, the phenomenon of rapidly increasing dependency heavily concentrated in metropolitan areas and among ethnic minorities who displayed additionally the stigmata of social disorganization—high crime rates, illegitimacy, broken homes, and educational failure—was both unexpected and unacceptable.

Work or welfare became an option for large segments of the poverty population rather than a dichotomy determined by external circumstances over which the individual exercised little control, and this option symbolized the confusion over the direction of social welfare policy. The question of employability became a major issue, compelling a reexamination of old assumptions about the relation of public assistance beneficiaries to the labor market; an analysis of the employment effects of the current welfare structure; and the initiation of strategems to replace dependency with labor-market participation. A review of the development of the welfare dilemma and of the experience with alterations in the assistance programs should sharpen our understanding both of the nexus between work and welfare and of the critical questions which must inform any effective reform effort.

The income-maintenance function under the Social Security Act is performed through four programs: (1) Old Age, Survivors, Disability, and Health Insurance (OASDHI), which is most commonly identified as "social security"; (2) Unemployment Insurance Benefits (UIB); (3) the recently enacted Supplemental Security Income (SSI), which as of 1974 provides income to the aged, the blind, and the disabled who lack OASDHI coverage or receive inadequate benefits; and (4) Aid to Families with Dependent Children (AFDC), which is usually identified as "welfare."

OASDHI provides nationally uniform benefits for the retired or disabled worker and his dependents or for the worker's survivors, whose eligibility is established by mandatory contributions made by the individual during his working years. While it is financed with taxes paid by the current work force and employers, it is popularly perceived as insurance with benefits proportional to contributions. During almost four decades of its existence, the program has expanded in range and comprehensiveness. Its benefits have been progressively liberalized, and in theory it has been considered a satisfactory model for the treatment of the full range of vicissitudes threatening a worker's self-support, assuming full employment at adequate earnings under a properly functioning economy. Its operation has been considered exemplary. The chief source of dissatisfaction, a current concern of students of public welfare and of the public budget, has been the method of financing. The payroll tax is regressive and places an inequitable burden upon the growing number of families with two workers. Significant increases in the tax base and rate in recent years have become onerous for low- and moderate-income families.

The UIB program is also an income-maintenance program for the employable population derived from social insurance. Benefits are related to prior earnings, and contributions are made through a payroll tax. However, specific eligibility criteria and benefit structure are not detailed in federal law (as they are in the case of OASDHI) but are left to the discretion of state governments. The result is a program which exempts from coverage many workers and whose duration and level of benefits are limited and variable. These provisions minimize the effectiveness of UIB for the poor.

In contrast to UIB and OASDHI, which are intended to serve the work force and their families, specific categorical assistance programs—Old Age Assistance (OAA), Aid to the Blind (AB), Aid to the Disabled (AD), and AFDC—were created under the Social Security Act to maintain unemployable groups. These programs were administered by state and local agencies and financed by state and local funds matched by federal general revenues. More importantly, eligibility required a means test, and acceptance procedures and benefit levels varied significantly according to administrative jurisdiction, characteristically the state. Replacement of the "adult" categories (OAA, AB, and AD) with the SSI program in 1974 created a federally administered system with minimum national benefits financed from federal revenues and thereby eliminated many of the inequities and inconsistencies of the categorical programs. Presently AFDC remains the single "welfare" program under the Social Security Act.

Since over 90 percent of the heads of AFDC families are mothers, they traditionally have been included among the unemployable, reflecting the conceptions and circumstances of the 1930s—

the assumed beneficial effects for children of the mother's presence at home; the exigencies of the labor market of the depression; and the low labor-force participation rates of married women (about 15 percent in the thirties as compared with 40 percent in 1970). Employable adults other than mothers of young children have been consistently excluded from federally reimbursable assistance, and their treatment has been left completely at the discretion of the individual states. The extension of AFDC to two-parent families with an unemployed father (AFDC-U), legislated in 1961, is a voluntary program which, as of 1973, had been adopted by only 24 jurisdictions. Other than state-financed general assistance (Home Relief) in the more liberal states, there are no support programs for the "working poor," the intact family whose head is underemployed or the underemployed individual. Legislative proposals sent by President Nixon to the Ninety-first and Ninety-second Congresses would have provided support for poor families with children through a combined minimum-income guarantee and earnings incentive, but their failure of enactment has perpetuated the *status quo ante*.

The "withering away" doctrine of social welfare theory viewed public assistance as a residual program whose function would gradually disappear with the expansion of social insurance programs. This doctrine persisted unchanged throughout the fifties, with little in the program statistics to challenge it. Despite a progressively aging poulation, the number of OAA and AB recipients actually declined between 1950 and 1970, by 25 percent and 18 percent, respectively, reflecting enhancement of the original OASDHI in both coverage and benefit levels. It should be recalled that assistance for the aged was the primary intent of the writers of the original Social Security Legislation and constituted numerically the largest of the categorical programs until the late fifties, when it was exceeded by AFDC. Until 1966 AFDC underwent modest expansion: its growth rates were not incommensurate with the increase in the number of children in the total population. In fact, the first half of the fifties actually saw a reduction in the number of AFDC cases and recipients.[1]

Dislodgment of the "withering away" doctrine by sheer weight of numbers did not occur until the latter half of the sixties, when national annual rates of increase in the recipient population

4

reached 20 percent (1969) and eventually peaked at 32 percent (1970). However, evidence for the dysfunction of AFDC had surfaced earlier in the form of rising indices of family disorganization and worsening social conditions among the dependent poor, for whom the program had originally been devised to lend a measure of social and economic stability. These twin factors of qualitative deterioration and quantitative expansion with respect to AFDC recipients were dramatized by the concurrent phenomenon of an incontrovertible decrease in the nation's poverty population.

The assumed dichotomy between labor-force participants and unemployables underlying the structural dualism of the Social Security System, OASDHI and UIB versus categorical public assistance, was also challenged during the 1960s. With the declaration of a War on Poverty, attention focused on AFDC, which constituted the base and the bulk of the nation's antipoverty effort, and study findings suggested alternative conceptualizations of the program and its beneficiaries.

One corollary of the traditional view of adults on the AFDC rolls as mothers whose childcare responsibilities make them unemployable is the perception of a static caseload. Since dependency is attributed to extra-labor-market factors little affected by general economic trends, welfare status is expected to be continuous over a long period of time, with minimal mobility for the female head of household. Empirical investigation tended to reveal the unexpected: episodic dependency of relatively short median duration (approximately two years); substantial caseload fluidity with annual turnover rates averaging one-third; recidivism rates ranging from one-third to 40 percent; and a predictable frequency of openings and closings caused by changes in employment status.[2] Surveys reported both substantial work histories for AFDC mothers and a distinct subset who had worked immediately before and/or concurrently with the receipt of assistance.[3]

From all of these findings there emerged a revised conception of a dynamic AFDC population, considerably larger than the number actually receiving assistance at any one time. For this extensive population at risk, it was hypothesized that earnings from employment interweave in diverse temporal and structural patterns with welfare grants for the production of income. Some recipients alternate between employment and assistance sporadically or seasonally; others combine income from both sources simultaneously, licitly or illicitly; still others resort to public assistance in the event of failure of their extremely marginal resources during modest downswings in the economy. The dependent population was seen to be coextensive with the larger poverty population, and empiric investigation has tended to deny distinctions between the dependent and the working poor.

Statements concerning the employment status of welfare recipients and policy recommendations based upon such assessments have been drawn from studies of the movement of persons on and off welfare, analyses of reasons for acceptance and termination and of durations of episodic assistance, and examinations of the frequency and temporal patterns of recidivism. Many of these have been national studies utilizing aggregate data, so that what has emerged has been a general picture of an irregularly employed worker loosely attached to a poorly paying labor market against whose vicissitudes public assistance provides a bolster.

But if the adult welfare recipient is essentially a marginal member of the labor force, then the other side of the coin to be assayed is the labor market in which he participates. This aspect has only begun to be investigated through poverty area studies and a series of small-sample in-depth, or participatory, efforts.[4] Accordingly, much is known of the characteristics of the welfare recipient, but there is little detailed information on the labor market in which he works intermittently or has worked in the past and to which he will perforce return unless deterred by external causes. In light of the recent legislative emphasis upon employment of adult AFDC recipients, which has been articulated in the work incentive (WIN) provisions of the Social Security Amendments of 1967 and reinforced by the Talmadge Amendment of 1971, and of the essentially local nature of the labor market for marginal workers, any programmatic effort must address itself to the local scene. Pragmatism dictates knowledge of the work experience of the public assistance population, not only in its temporal dimensions but in its substantive dimensions as well; the industries whose work forces may shift to welfare seasonally, cyclically, or secularly; their wages and other conditions of employment; and their place in the local economy.

This study was undertaken to ascertain the interaction of work and welfare in the lives of public assistance recipients through actual case-record review, not inferentially from aggregate statistics. For a detailed examination of the dynamics of the welfare system, its relation to the local economy, and the employment behavior of the welfare population, we have selected New York City. Like most large cities, New York experienced the "welfare explosion" of the 1960s, and the demographic, political, economic, and administrative changes which have, individually and collectively, been held responsible are all present. Administrative responsibility for New York's public assistance program is vested in the municipal government, which acts within the statutory authority granted by the state legislature and administrative guidelines set forth by the state Department of Social Services. The city's Human Resources Administration executes the AFDC, AFDC-U, and Home Relief programs and, prior to enactment of SSI, also administered the OAA, AB, and AD programs. Until 1971 this function was carried out in over 40 separate offices, commonly called "welfare centers," located throughout the city and staffed by civil servants, who served as caseworkers. Since then, the granting of benefits has been separated from social services; the former is conducted in a large network of "income-maintenance centers," primarily by clerks, while the latter are performed in "community-service centers" by caseworkers.

New York City's economy is highly diversified, including a relatively large proportion of service and other nonmanufacturing industries, as well as a varied manufacturing sector providing almost 700,000 jobs. During the latter half of the 1960s employment expanded rapidly in the private and public service sectors, more than compensating for contractions in manufacturing; but in 1969 job declines began, and total losses since then have offset the gains of the 1960s.[5] These job losses were accompanied, paradoxically, by a decline in labor-force participation rates from 57 percent in 1969 (a rate already below the national average) to less than 55 percent in 1973 and by a decrease in the number counted as unemployed because of those not actively seeking work.[6]

The magnitude of New York's dependency problem may be grasped from a few figures. In a numerically stable population of approximately 8 million, the number of dependents rose from 328,000 in 1960 to 1.2 million in 1970, or from 4 percent of the city's inhabitants to 15 percent. In terms of household heads, the comparable numbers are 137,000 and 454,000 of a total adult population (aged 18 and over) that grew only minimally from 5.6 million to 5.7 million over the same period of time. The 318,000 adults (aged 18 to 65) on the AFDC, AFDC-U, and HR caseloads in 1970 comprised nearly 7 percent of the 4.6 million New Yorkers in the same age group. In relation to the city's total work force of almost 3.3 million the percentage is higher, but the base is not completely comparable, since it includes individuals below age 18 and over age 65.[7] Obviously, the manpower loss is considerable.[8]

In terms of any strategem for reform, the relationship of this segment of the welfare population to the local labor market is critical: Should government intervention continue to be directed toward individual motivation to work, the principle underlying the Work Incentive (WIN) Amendments, the Talmadge Amendment, and President Nixon's unsuccessful reform efforts? If, as has been hypothesized by dual-labor-market theorists,[9] adult welfare recipients represent a peripheral labor force to meet the requirements of marginal industries and establishments, or a labor reserve, then welfare grants may be considered to serve a covert subsidizing function vis-à-vis this subeconomy. Is this compensatory device the strategem of choice for correcting labor-market malfunction? Alternatively, if the current welfare structure, along with multiple in-kind benefits, discourages low-wage employment, is welfare reform or a wage policy the appropriate governmental response to the present dilemma? Is self-support or employment with wage supplementation a reasonable goal for the resolution of the present unacceptably high rate of welfare dependency?

This study examines the work experience and work-welfare relationships of a sample of New York public assistance recipients. The next chapter explains how the sample was selected and describes the personal characteristics of the welfare recipients: sex, race, origin, age, marital status, number of dependent children, years of schooling, and the incidence of such problems as physical and mental illness, drug and alcohol addiction, police records, and child-related difficulties. Much of the subsequent analysis is conducted through the "filters" of these personal characteristics.

Chapter 3 offers an analysis of the complete public assistance history of the sample in terms of temporal distribution of public assistance episodes, duration of episodes, opening reasons, and, where applicable, closing reasons. Chapter 4 presents the current employment status of the sample and analyzes the differences among those working, those not working but looking for work, and those neither working nor looking for work. This chapter also examines the work history of those in the sample who previously had been jobholders in order to determine the duration of that employment.

In chapter 5 the nature of the jobs held both currently and formerly by the welfare sample is analyzed in terms of industry, occupation, wage rate, and duration. Changes over time in the characteristics of the jobs held by the group are also examined. Chapter 6 reports on a follow-up study of the group 17 months after the initial histories were obtained. Included in the follow-up are subsequent changes in dependency status and the relationship of these changes to employment behavior. The final chapter summarizes the findings and presents the policy implications of the study, as well as suggestions for further research.

2

The Sample

Labor-force potential and labor-force experience are to no small extent related to personal characteristics; accordingly, it is essential to determine whether and in what respect a city's welfare population differs from the population at large and to define systematic variation among recipient subsets. This chapter will describe sample selection and the rationale for stratification and will analyze the personal characteristics of the sample population. Additionally, the presence of specific personal problems relevant to dependency and employability, such as physical and mental disability, alcoholism, narcotics addiction, and police records, will be reviewed.

Structure of the Sample

The initial design of the investigation proposed in 1969 called for an intensive small-sample, case-record study by a group of trained researchers who, in addition to gathering the required data, would be able to evaluate the quality of individual work experience on the basis of predetermined criteria. However, in the unsettled climate resulting from the joint federal-state special review of the New York City AFDC program (1968–69) and subsequent state reviews of the operations of the Department of Social Services (DOSS) as a whole, another exposure of departmental records to external scrutiny was not feasible; additionally, the nonofficial status of the investigators raised questions of propriety. To obviate these difficulties, the procedure was revised as a joint endeavor with the DOSS, utilizing caseworkers for the case-record search and our own staff for data analysis. Sample size was enlarged to 2,000, and it was planned that each questionnaire would be completed by the caseworker assigned to the individual member of the sample, since familiarity with the case presumed greater accuracy of reportage, although it might constitute a source of bias. Unfortunately, local political unease and ongoing departmental changes in staff and operations delayed the actual commencement of the survey for over a year, in the course of which separation of the social-services function from income maintenance was implemented in accordance with HEW mandate and traditional caseloads were dissolved. Ultimately questionnaires were completed by caseworkers in the respective welfare centers from which the sample members were drawn, who were, however, unlikely to be familiar with the individual case.

Given the difficulty of access to data, compromises were necessary. Pre-testing was not possible, and considerable variability in the quality of response made vigorous editing necessary. Over 300 incomplete and internally inconsistent questionnaires were eliminated, reducing the usable sample to 1,698. Compromises were also dictated by time. Between late 1969, when the study was conceptualized, and its implementation in 1971, economic conditions both nationwide and in New York had deteriorated. Consequently, opportunities for employment among the currently dependent population were seriously limited at the time the sample was drawn, and conceivably behavioral patterns selected for observation were therefore distorted. On the other hand, this situation led to the expectation that the data would provide a view of the responsiveness of public assistance to economic recession and that differential welfare-utilization patterns would emerge.

Fortunately, supplementary data became available, indicating the presence or absence of members of the sample on the active caseload at the close of July 1973 and the reasons for termination of those cases that had been closed in the interim. Additionally, reopenings during the period January 1972–May 1973 were retrieved from DOSS data. Extension of the temporal base of the survey permitted preliminary identification of the variables affecting welfare mobility.

Since the primary objective of the study was to examine the interaction of dependency and labor-force participation, the sample was limited to three of the six categories of assistance provided in New York City as of 1971—Home Relief (HR), AFDC, and AFDC-U. Recipients of OAA, AB, and AD were excluded from the sample because they were presumed to have the least employment potential and their work-welfare relationships were less relevant to current policy issues. Federalization of these categories through the SSI program more than two years after the initial research design may be viewed as a confirmation of this judgment.

Because of the emphasis on past and potential employment, the sample was structured to include a large number of male household heads so that this group could be studied in greater depth than random sampling of the delimited caseload was likely to permit. In order to include a sufficient number of adult male recipients, the AFDC-U and HR categories were overrepresented, constituting two-fifths of the total study population in contrast to one-quarter of all HR, AFDC, and AFDC-U cases on the New York City caseload as of September 1971, the month of sample selection.

A particular subset selected for representation in the sample was that of AFDC mothers whose youngest dependent child reached the age of 18 in 1971. Although they represent a small proportion of the caseload, these women, whose eligibility for federally reimbursable assistance was nearing termination and who had been long freed of major childcare responsibilities, might be considered potential labor-force participants. They number 273, constituting 16 percent of the entire sample and 24 percent of all female household heads.

The overrepresentation of two groups with presumably high employment potential—adult males, and females whose youngest child is 17 or 18 years old—must constantly be kept in mind so the study population will not be taken as a representative sample of the entire caseload. Throughout the analysis we have sought to present separately findings for three subgroups within the welfare population—male household heads, AFDC mothers whose youngest child is aged 18, and all other female household heads. In instances where the two latter groups could be combined without distorting the findings, data are analyzed by sex only. We have not sought to use aggregate data from the sample as representative of the welfare population as a whole, and our findings should be interpreted as relevant only to the work and welfare experience of the particular subgroup or subgroups investigated. In light of the well-known differences in employment behavior by sex, this subdivision of the sample was presumed to be useful in the illumination of the dynamics of work and welfare, which was the primary focus of the study.

Personal Characteristics

Personal characteristics, such as age, ethnicity, educational attainment, and origin (migrant or native), are obviously related to employability. Data relating to these characteristics of the household heads in the welfare sample and comparable figures for the total adult population of New York City are presented in table 2.1.

Several conspicuous differences emerge when the three welfare groups are compared with the general adult population. The widely publicized overrepresentation of ethnic minorities on the public assistance rolls is replicated in the sample. Although whites and others are approximately 70 percent of the total New York adult population, they comprise only about one-fifth of each welfare group. Most striking is the pervasive economic deprivation of Puerto Ricans. A mere 9 percent of all adults in the city, they constitute more than half the male welfare family heads, 46 percent of AFDC female household heads with a youngest child aged 18, and 36 percent of other female heads of welfare families.

Not surprisingly, the welfare household heads have less education than the general adult population. Although over half the total adult population of the city have completed high school, the comparable figure for male heads of welfare families is only one-fifth, and for most female family heads it is less than one-quarter. Among the group of AFDC mothers with a youngest child aged eighteen the proportion is about one-tenth. The low educational attainment of the welfare sample does not appear to be solely a function of the group's ethnic mix. A more detailed comparison of the educational levels of welfare household heads and the general

Table 2.1   Selected Personal Characteristics of Welfare-Sample Household Heads and New York Adults (in percent)

| Personal characteristics | Welfare-sample household heads | | | N.Y. adults[a] | |
	Male	Female with youngest dependent child aged 18	All other females	Male	Female
Age	(542)	(269)	(863)		
18–24	14	—	15	19	19
25–34	31	3	31	23	22
35–44	26	34	25	20	19
45–64	29	63	29	38	40
Ethnitcity	(511)	(247)	(820)		
Puerto Rican	51	46	36	9	9
Black	29	32	44	19	21
White and other	20	22	20	72	70
Origin	(539)	(270)	(860)		
Migrant	80	86	76	44	46
Native	20	14	24	56	54
Educational attainment	(366)	(160)	(595)		
Less than high school	46	61	39	20	21
Some high school	34	28	38	20	19
High-school graduate	15	9	18	29	39
Post-high school	5	2	5	31	22

SOURCE: U.S., Bureau of the Census, *Census of Population: 1970. Detailed Characteristics*, Final Report PQ(1)-D34.

NOTES: Response rates for welfare-sample groups: age and origin, 99 percent; ethnicity, 93 percent; educational attainment, 66 percent. Figures in parentheses represent absolute numbers.

[a] Data are for New York City residents aged 16 to 64, except for the category "educational attainment," where percentages apply to New York SMSA residents aged 20 to 64.

adult population by sex and ethnicity reveals that the former primarily represent the least-educated segment of each ethnic minority (see table 2.2). For example, two-thirds of the Puerto Rican females in the sample had only an elementary school education, while of the total adult female Puerto Rican population in the New York metropolitan area, this was true for only half. Similarly, in each of the sex-race groupings in table 2.2 welfare household heads are significantly overrepresented in the lower educational categories.

The educational deprivation of the welfare groups appears to be even more severe when their high degree of migrancy is taken into

Table 2.2 Educational Attainment of Welfare Sampl
Adult Population, New York SMSA, by Sex and Ethnicity

| Educational attainment | Females | | Welfa |
	Welfare sample	N.Y. adults	sampl
Puerto Ricans			
Less than high school	67	51	61
Some high school	24	25	29
High-school graduate	7	21	7
Post-high school	1	4	2
Blacks			
Less than high school	36	26	34
Some high school	41	28	39
High-school graduate	19	35	24
Post-high school	4	12	4
Whites and others			
Less than high school	29	17	33
Some high school	41	17	35
High-school graduate	23	41	19
Post-high school	8	25	13

SOURCE: U.S., Bureau of the Census, *Census of Population: 1970. D*
Characteristics, Final Report PC(1)-D34.

NOTE: Response rate: 62 percent. Ages of welfare-sample household
range from 18 to 64; of adults, New York SMSA, from 20 to 64.

account. Four-fifths of the male welfare household heads w
born outside New York State, as compared with less than half
the city's total adult male population. Among the female welfar
sample groups a substantial overrepresentation of migrants is als
evident. Additional analysis of the sample data indicated that 84
percent of all the migrants arrived in New York at age 18 or older,
and in these cases it is assumed that their education was acquired
in their region of birth.[1] In the case of the Puerto Ricans, almost
all of whom are migrants, and of the blacks, who are only somewhat less so, the quantitative meagerness of their schooling is exacerbated by the relative dysfunction of southern and Puerto Rican
schooling for New York City labor-force participation.

The age distribution of household heads in the sample groups
points to the not unexpected finding that AFDC mothers with a
youngest child aged 18 tend to be older than the other females.
Nearly two-thirds are over 45, and only 3 percent are under 35. In
contrast, compared with their distribution in the general adult

pulation, male household heads and other females in the sample
somewhat overrepresented in the prime employment age
oups. However, it should be noted that the figures for the general
opulation include all adults, not only household heads, and there-
re a large proportion of younger adults (between the ages of 18
nd 24) who are not in independent households.

Educational achievement is closely associated with age. Two-
hirds of the older males and females (aged 45 to 64) lack any
high-school education, in contrast to only one-tenth of the females
and one-fifth of the males in the youngest age group (aged 18 to
24). However, much of the improvement in educational achievement in the younger cohorts is merely a shift from less than high
school to some high school, with little change, particularly among
males, in the proportion of individuals having a high-school diploma or better. Four out of five of the youngest males and seven
out of ten of the youngest females lack a high-school diploma—
proportions strikingly similar to those for older males (82 percent) although lower than those for older females (89 percent).

Analysis of the three sample groups by age and ethnicity reveals
a general pattern of older whites (aged 45 to 64) and younger
minorities (under 35). Differences between the age distributions of
the two minority groups, blacks and Puerto Ricans, are slight,
except in the case of female family heads with a youngest child
aged 18. Among these women, the higher proportion of older
whites and Puerto Ricans suggests the presence of larger families,
or alternatively an earlier childbearing age for blacks.

Family Composition

Family structure and size classically are cited as the basic deter-
rents to self-support of public assistance recipients, and in fact
abnormal family structure constitutes the condition of eligibility
for the largest and most problematic program, AFDC. An examination of the data reveals that four-fifths of male recipients are
heads of intact families, while two-thirds of all females have suf-
fered marital breakup.

The stereotype of predominantly large families among the dependent population is not confirmed by the sample data. Excluding
the group selected with a youngest child aged 18, only 18 percent

of the families with female heads and 23 percent of those with male heads had four or more children. Approximately one-fifth of both male and female heads had no dependent children, and an additional 20 percent and 25 percent, respectively, had only one child.

For females, both age and number of children must be considered in assessing employability. Below is the percent distribution of female household heads, excluding those whose youngest child is 18, in terms of dependent children and their ages:

Number and ages of dependent children	*Percent*
None	20
None under 6, one or two over 6	24
One under 6	11
Two under 6	6
None under 6, three or more over	14
One under 6, one or two over	10
All others	15

The figures indicate a relatively large proportion of female-headed households with limited childcare responsibilities. In addition to one-fifth with no children, almost one-quarter have no children under age 6 and only one or two school-age children. If these two groups are combined with those having only one child under 6, 55 percent of the sample might be free of childcare responsibilities with modest supportive services. However, this assessment must be interpreted cautiously, for other problems may be present which make employment difficult or impossible.

Problems of Welfare Household Heads

Underlying income-maintenance programs is the definition of the recipients' needs primarily in financial terms. Certainly this was true of the programs mandated under the original Social Security legislation. In the case, however, of public assistance beneficiaries, this perception has undergone considerable change and, beginning in the 1950s, has been replaced by the view that AFDC families in particular are disproportionately beset by social problems that are not amenable to financial resolution alone. Both the social-service programs of the early sixties and the manpower-development programs of the latter half of the decade are rooted in this conception. Accordingly, considerable attention has been focused upon the detection and identification of problems, with the implicit assumption that such data may provide clues to the understanding of the welfare dynamic.

Unlike the data that have been reviewed thus far, responses to questionnaire items concerning individual problems were to a great degree based upon the subjective judgment of the caseworker who reviewed the individual record, which is, itself, a reflection of the subjective judgment of caseworkers who handled the case. Except for a query regarding police records, questions about specified and unspecified disabilities were clearly subject to reporter bias, and analysis of the findings of necessity must be cautious. With this caveat, we turn to the data describing the incidence of various problems among the sample groups.

Problems were reported for almost two-fifths of the male household heads, about half of the females with a youngest child aged 18, and nearly a third of the other females. Chronic physical illness was by far the most common problem, present among 30 percent of the males, 43 percent of the females with a child aged 18, and 23 percent of the other females, while mental illness, including addiction and alcoholism, was relatively infrequent. Very few household heads were reputed to be illiterate or to have some other language problem. Six percent of the males, but hardly any females, were reported as having some criminal record. Family-related problems, which most commonly referred to special child-care needs, were reported for almost one-fifth of the other females and typically were related to the number of children requiring care. The incidence of such problems corresponds to the number of families with four or more children. The presence of family-related problems among mothers with a youngest child aged 18 suggests that women in this group are burdened with particularly troublesome children (retarded or disabled, for example) or are providing care for grandchildren or other extended-family members.

If the welfare sample appears unremarkable in terms of the frequency of specified problems, except for the high incidence of reported but unspecified chronic physical illness, it is distinguished

18

by the large number of "multi-problem families" revealed in the brief comments concerning individual welfare cases appended by the respondent caseworkers. Since the selection of additional information for inclusion was completely discretionary, no attempt was made to subject the content of the comments to statistical analysis. They do, however, convey vividly the nature of the difficulties and the quality of life experienced by a substantial segment of the welfare population. A dozen of the more problematic, although not necessarily atypical, caseworker comments follow:

1. The family consists of a man and a woman in their late fifties with a teenage daughter. The husband spent most of his adult life in prison and presently suffers from mental difficulties, which make him incommunicative and vague. He has attempted suicide on several occasions. Mrs. L. supported the family until a turn in her back forced her to quit work, as it hampered the use of her left arm. The daughter is a high-school graduate who does well enough in school to be considered for the SEEK program.

2. The client is the mother of ten children. She was married twice. Both husbands are deceased. She supported herself and her children from employment as a domestic until she injured her leg in December 1970.

3. Although Mr. V. for the most part worked until 1/70 (short-term jobs), it is to be noted that he is a very heavy drinker. This has caused a great deal of tension and friction in the home and has made Mrs. V., who is asthmatic, quite nervous. Aside from this problem, their oldest daughter (not in family composition) has had two out-of-wedlock babies, who are cared for by Mrs. V.; and the oldest son was truant a lot from school and has also been found in possession of drugs.

4. The family consists of a middle-aged couple with a teenage daughter. Mr. O. is 59 and in a genarally run-down condition. His primary employment has been as a building maintenance man and super. His employer has been either unable or unwilling to employ him on a full-time basis. Mrs. O. is arthritic. Her husband has had to take over her duties as super of building in which they reside to maintain free

rent. The daughter dropped out of school in ninth grade—
she has never worked.

5. This family consists of 7 people. The husband has been disabled since the fall of 1967. Two of the 5 children are retarded. The wife was forced to leave her job because of
family responsibilities. The wife is noted in the case record
as being very competent and resourceful, but it is not likely
that she would become eligible for employment.

6. The client lives alone and was separated from her husband,
who is now in prison. He was a professional burglar. The
client has not worked in over 20 years. She was a secretary.
We do not know how long she worked. At the present time
the client does not appear to be a suitable candidate for employment. Her right arm was severely burned several years
ago, and as a result of a head injury received after she was
beaten up by her husband's friend, she has been suffering
seizures. She is under psychiatric care. Although the doctors
have recommended light manual employment, she is not
motivated to work due to her emotional condition.

7. Mr. E. has had a very irregular employment history. He has
been under psychiatric care diagnosed as reactive depression.
Basic complaints of fatigue, nervousness, and irritability persist. Mrs. E., Bill, and Ruth are also under psychiatric care;
the second son is in placement away from home.

8. Mr. F. often misses days at work because of illness. He has
had TB, which is arrested, but he is still not in very good
health. Because of absence he is often laid off from his job.
Mr. F. has a drinking problem, which interferes with his
employment.

9. Miss C. was in foster care since the age of 14, she could not
get along with parents. She worked before giving birth to an
out-of-wedlock child. She was hospitalized at Mt. Sinai in
1965 for psychiatric reasons. She was enrolled in a WIN
program but dropped out because of childcare and health
reasons.

10. The family has worked at odd jobs, such as fortunetelling,
but they have never lived in one place long enough to establish a work history. They speak little English and have no
formal training. Mr. M. has a verified chronic back ailment.

11. The client is a middle-aged American male with an eighth-grade education. Previous caseworkers have indicated high intelligence despite limited education. The client has never married and has no relatives. The case record indicates apparent social isolation. The client has lived in a series of furnished rooms. Over the past five years, and most of his prior life, the client supported himself by day work, usually in the restaurant field. His lack of skills and education is complicated by recurring skin infections on both legs, for which he has been hospitalized in the past.

12. Mrs. T. was living with her mother, who was also a public assistance recipient, when she was accepted for assistance at the age of 18. She has had three children: Rebecca (born 1963), Margaret (born 1964), and Ellen (born 1965) by a Mr. G., who never lived with her but did visit. Being usually in jail, he was unable to support. The first child was born when Mrs. T. was 16 years old. Since being on her own she has had constant problems with money management, with occasional utility shutoffs and eviction. In 1970 she informed us that she had married Mr. G. (the father of the children) in 1967, and he was going to live in the home. He did for a few months until they had a fight, and she had him locked up again. The courts took Ellen away from her in 1970, as the child had been battered and burned by her. A sister-in-law has the child now. Mrs. T. is not interested in work training, as any program offered is "too boring."

Summary

A review of the personal and family characteristics of the sample yields the following profiles. Male household heads are overwhelmingly migrants of prime working age with less than a high-school education. Their families are intact and not abnormally large; over three-quarters have fewer than four children. The men tend to be members of minority groups, with Puerto Ricans in the majority. About one-third of the males suffer from a chronic illness, but relatively few have significant other problems.

Females selected because they were apparently free of childcare responsibilities (their youngest child is aged 18) are characterized by other traits which may limit employability. The majority are above age 45, and few have a high-school diploma. Moreover, nearly half of these women have some special problem, typically a chronic illness.

Other female household heads are predominantly migrants with limited education. However, they are relatively young and have few special problems. For a large proportion of these mothers, childcare responsibilities are either nonexistent or modest.

3

The Welfare Record

The macrostatistics of New York City's welfare caseload are well-known, specifically its escalation from an average of 125,000 cases in 1961 to just under 500,000 in 1971, representing 346,000 and 1.2 million individual recipients, respectively.[1] But the behavior of these cases subsequent to acceptance is considerably more obscure. This has led to the formulation of mutually contradictory conceptions ranging from the static "dependent forever" theory to the "revolving door" hypothesis, neither of which is wholly true or false.

This chapter is an effort to illuminate welfare behavior through a detailed analysis of the complete case histories of the sample, dating from initial acceptance to November 1971, approximately two months following sample selection. Each case history was reviewed in terms of the number, duration, and precipitants of episodes of dependency. In light of the primary objective of the study, to illuminate the work-welfare nexus, variables have been selected for their relevance to employment and employability.

The Evidence of Caseload Dynamics

A variety of statistical studies conducted during the 1960s—local and national—examined several aspects of welfare history and inferred a significant degree of caseload fluidity. The evidence falls into three categories: (1) recidivism, or the proportion of current cases that have previously received assistance; (2) duration, or the period of time during which a case is continuously receiving assistance; and (3) turnover, or the share of the total caseload that enters or leaves the rolls during a given time period. High rates of recidivism, short duration, and extensive turnover have been cited to illustrate the dynamic nature of the welfare caseload.

National statistics developed for AFDC by the Bureau of Family Services of the Welfare Administration and, subsequently, the Social and Rehabilitation Service of the Department of Health, Education, and Welfare (HEW) throughout the sixties indicated a repeater status for at least one-third of all cases, rising from 33 percent in 1961 to a maximum of 39 percent in 1967 and declining to 34 percent in 1971.[2] Local surveys, particularly of metropolitan areas, disclosed even higher rates of recidivism. A very high rate, 75 percent, was demonstrated by a study of the caseload in the state of Washington in 1964.[3] New York State, whose AFDC recipients predominantly reside in New York City, showed a repeat rate of 50 percent in 1961, which subsequently declined to 47 percent in 1969 and 39 percent in 1971.[4] The marked decrease in 1970–71 reflects the large-scale inflow of new recipients attributable to the economic recession.

Caseload turnover, the termination of some cases and their replacement by others, has given additional support to the concept of an ever changing welfare population. An illustrative study in one major eastern city found that of the total AFDC recipients during a six-year period prior to 1966 only 7 percent had been continuous recipients and that 75 percent more families received AFDC than had been on the rolls in any single year.

Turning specifically to New York City, recent studies undertaken by the Office of Policy Research of the Human Resources Administration in collaboration with the New York City–Rand Institute have analyzed both long- and short-term dynamics of the local caseload over a period of six years, 1967–72, and for a single calendar year, 1972.[5] Both examinations revealed a substantial excess in the total caseload over the number at any one point in time and thus over the number of cases receiving assistance continuously throughout the period. Over the long term, there were 90 percent more individual cases than the largest number in any one month and 55 percent more than the comparable

24

number for any one year; over the short term, the difference between total number of cases and highest number for any one
month was 20 percent. With respect to recidivism, analysis of all
cases opened during the period February–June 1967 found almost
40 percent to have closed and reopened at least once by December
1972, almost six years later.

The length of time the average case has been receiving assistance, as well as the length of time assistance has been received
prior to the current opening, have served as supplementary indices
of caseload fluidity, substantial turnover being associated with welfare episodes of shorter duration. During the 1960s national data
revealed consistently that about 30 percent of the AFDC caseload
was of less than one year's duration. This figure rose to 35 percent
in 1971—another reflection of the large number of accessions in
the wake of the 1970 recession. Similarly during the 1960s the
median duration of current openings remained stable at approximately two years, falling, as would be anticipated from the increased rate of accessions, to 1.6 years in 1971.[6] Termination
studies would produce figures representing longer average duration
and perhaps more realistic, since the data are not unduly influ-
enced by the inclusion of the most recent enrollments; however,
there has been a paucity of examinations of closed cases, and the
primary continuing data sources, HEW statistics, are derived from
current caseloads.

Analysis of welfare dynamics based upon official statistics of
openings, closings, and reopenings assumes a correspondence between these events and the occurrence of need, its termination, and
its subsequent recurrence in the lives of the recipients. Findings of
caseload fluidity are supposed to reflect the unstable economy of
the poor, which is rooted partly in substandard employment and
partly in dependency. The adequacy of this theory will be considered in the light of the sample which forms the basis of this study,
but at the outset it is important to clarify the actual meaning of the
statistics. Examination of the official administrative codes assigned
to reasons for opening and closing reveals that, while the occurrence of need is the necessary precipitant for welfare acceptance,
welfare termination is not necessarily need-related. In fact, the
majority of closings are for administrative reasons, reflecting non-
compliance by recipients with changing rules and regulations, and

others are for loss of contact, which gives no clue to the recipient's economic status. A large proportion of these are reopened shortly after being closed. The study of the day-by-day activity of the New York welfare caseload for the year 1972 performed by the Office of Policy Research (HRA) and the New York City–Rand Institute found a high proportion of short-run reopenings following administrative and lost-contact closings, and therefore all closings that ever led to a reopening coded "closed in error" or that resulted in a reopening for administrative reasons within 30 days were systematically classified as spurious. Accordingly, estimates of welfare mobility based uncritically upon administrative statistics, particularly closings and closing reasons, are suspect. A review of the questionnaire responses convincingly demonstrated that closings of 30 days or less were almost uniformly erroneous, disciplinary, or otherwise extraneous and that they in no sense indicated a change in need for public assistance. To eliminate this source of bias, these closings and the subsequent reopenings have been disregarded in our calculations.

Duration of Dependency

Analysis of data relating to duration of dependency, specifically year of first acceptance, total number of acceptances, and duration of current public assistance episode, yields several general findings and reveals important variations among the sample groups (see table 3.1). A critical finding is the fairly recent accession of most of the sample to the rolls. Among male household heads 40 percent were first accepted in 1970 or 1971, and a total of 73 percent were accepted from 1967 on. For the general category of females, 58 percent were first accepted from 1967 on. Only among females with a youngest dependent child aged 18 were a majority (62 percent) first accepted before 1967. Cross-sectional data from a sample drawn at a moment in time are necessarily biased by the inclusion of very recently added cases, but the stratification of our sample to include household heads with a youngest child aged 18 provides an opportunity both to examine the history of cases with longer records of dependency and also to investigate the more recently added population of male- and female-headed households.

There is little evidence of frequent alternation between depen-

Table 3.1   Public Assistance Record of Sample Groups (in percent)

Public assistance	Males	Females with youngest dependent child aged 18	All other females
Date of first acceptance	(543)	(270)	(872)
1932–67	26	62	42
1967–69	33	26	36
1970–71	40	12	22
Total number of acceptances	(544)	(272)	(877)
1	68	65	72
2	22	23	19
3	8	9	7
4 or more	3	3	2
Total time	(542)	(269)	(872)
Under 6 months	7	1	3
6–11 months	19	4	8
12–23 months	23	11	15
24–35 months	13	9	12
36–59 months	20	20	27
5–9 years	13	32	21
10 years or more	5	22	14
Duration of current episode	(541)	(270)	(873)
Under 6 months	12	2	6
6–11 months	20	6	9
12–23 months	24	13	16
24–35 months	13	9	12
36–59 months	17	23	27
5–9 years	9	29	20
10 years or more	4	19	10

NOTES: Figures in parentheses represent absolute numbers. Response rates range from 98 percent to 100 percent.

dency and self-support for any substantial fraction of recipients. In each group the overwhelming majority of cases are one-time acceptances, with an additional one-fifth having experienced two episodes; only about 10 percent had three or more acceptances. The predominance of single episodes of dependency in the sample is reflected in aggregate figures for the distribution of total public assistance duration and duration of current acceptance. Fifty-six percent of all cases in the sample have received welfare assistance for a total of three years or more, and 51 percent of all current episodes have been continuously open for three or more years.

It seems clear from the similarity of these distributions that very few of the current caseload utilized welfare as a buffer against intermittent employment. Even more suggestive is the fact that of all cases with a total duration of over ten years, 60 percent have been continuously on welfare, and 78 percent have received assistance continuously for the last ten years. Since at time of acceptance—1961 or earlier—these chronic cases represented a considerably greater proportion of the total caseload than they do today, it is apparent that for many, especially AFDC mothers, acceptance for welfare has signified long-term removal from the labor market. Unless the current caseload of predominantly recent accessions constitutes a different population, a large proportion of these, too, may persist as chronic dependents in the absence of programmatic countermeasures or significant external change. Since most of these chronic cases are families headed by females, perhaps the declining birth rate that has begun to affect the welfare population will diminish long-term dependency for the support of multi-child households.[7]

One might infer from the above summary that the caseload behaves uniformly; in fact there is considerable variability among groups (see table 3.1). Female-headed households are more likely to be dependent on public assistance for longer periods of time than male-headed households. Among the males only 5 percent may be characterized as "hard core," with total durations of ten years or more; for the two female samples the corresponding figures are 22 percent and 14 percent. If chronicity is defined as a current welfare episode of three years or longer, only 30 percent of male-headed households can be defined as chronically dependent, compared with 71 percent and 57 percent of the two female-headed-household groups.

Among female-headed households, the marital status of the head is related to duration of dependency. A division of the heads of all AFDC households into the categories (1) never married, (2) married—spouse present, and (3) married—spouse not present shows that women with a husband present had somewhat shorter periods of dependency than the others. One-third had received assistance for two years or less, in contrast to one-fourth of those who had never married and those whose husbands were no longer with the family. This is true despite the fact that by definition female-headed AFDC households may only have a spouse present if he is disabled or otherwise unemployable. (A female-headed household with children and an employable husband who is unemployed would be classified AFDC-U, and a female-headed household with a fully-employed spouse would be classified HR.) The presence of a spouse, even if he is unemployable, appears to curtail the duration of dependency for female-headed families.

The First Public Assistance Episode

Initial acceptances merit specific study for a variety of reasons. First, they provide clues to the character of the welfare population and the circumstances at the time the critical decision to seek assistance is made. Second, the relationship of these circumstances to subsequent welfare history may provide insights into the different patterns of dependency, ranging from long-term receipt of public assistance to short-term reliance in periods of acute need.

Examination of year of first acceptance revealed that, despite a range of 39 years, from 1932 to 1971, approximately 60 percent of the caseload was initially accepted in the period from 1967 on (see table 3.1). The period of initial accession to public assistance differed sharply by sex of household head. Three out of four male household heads first received welfare in 1967 or later, in contrast to more than one out of two females. Only one-tenth of the males antecede 1962, as compared with a quarter of the females. In fact, 6 percent of the latter first received assistance more than 20 years before the sampling date; only 1 percent of males go back as far.

In analyzing the circumstances of first acceptance, changes over time are of particular interest. To avoid the proliferation of small and empty cells in temporal distributions because of the wide span of years, the intervals preceding 1967 that contain 40 percent of the cases have been collapsed into one period, and the final five years have been divided into two periods, 1967–69 and 1970–71. There is more than a technical rationale to this subdivision: since these three periods correspond respectively to the pre-welfare-explosion years; the peak of the explosion and its brief abatement in 1969; and the economic recession, shifts relative to these events may be illuminated.

Caution is required in the interpretation of similarities and contrasts among these three time periods because they differ in their degree of representativeness. The 1970–71 group is most likely to reflect the total universe of first acceptances during that period; the 1967–69 sample is somewhat biased toward intermediate-range cases; the pre-1967 category reflects only long-term and intermittent welfare recipients who were initially accepted during that period. In a sense, our findings in this analysis of trends in first acceptances may be said to describe the characteristics and behavior of the current caseload differentiated by degree of chronicity.

Analysis of age at first acceptance indicates that females are slightly more likely to first seek assistance when they are under 25 than are males (see table 3.2). However, for recent years both sexes show higher ratio of early (under age 25) assistance and a decrease in the proportionate share of those first seeking assistance between the ages of 25 and 34. During 1970–71 the under-25 age group accounted for the largest proportion of all female accessions and the second largest proportion of male accessions. In addition, the proportion of females over 44 who were first accepted doubled after 1967 and was only slightly short of the rate of the under-25 age group in 1970–71. In sum, the greatest relative increase in new acceptances has been among the youngest males and females and oldest females.

Although use of the same time periods to analyze the ethnic distribution of persons first accepted masks shifts that took place

Table 3.2 Age of Welfare Household Heads at Date of First Acceptance, by Sex (in percent)

	Date of first acceptance		
Age	Before 1967	1967–69	1970–71
Males	(141)	(180)	(219)
Under 25	19	18	28
25–34	43	38	33
35–44	20	23	19
Over 44	18	21	21
Females	(529)	(376)	(218)
Under 25	27	24	30
25–34	39	27	26
35–44	21	22	17
Over 44	13	27	27

NOTES: Response rate: 98 percent. Figures in parentheses represent absolute numbers.

in the 1950s and early 1960s, specifically the growing number of blacks and then Puerto Ricans, it permits a detailed examination of more recent trends. In the period of the welfare explosion, 1967–69, the proportion of Puerto Rican females first accepted for assistance rose, as did the proportion of white and "other" males. During these years, Puerto Ricans comprised the largest ethnic group among newly accepted household heads—56 percent of all males, 42 percent of all females. White and other males increased their share from 10 percent before 1967 to 27 percent, while both black males and black females showed a relative decline. The 1970–71 recession witnessed the greatest increase in the share of whites accepted for assistance: roughly one-fifth of total first acceptances in this period were white males and females.

Precipitants for Seeking Assistance

The interaction between labor-force participation and public assistance as alternative sources of income may be estimated in the first instance from an analysis of the official reasons for case opening. The reasons for initial acceptance were classified among five categories, in accordance with the objective of isolating those precipitants representing loss of earning power from other causes of financial need:

1) health—illness, injury, or other disability of the household head;
2) job loss—loss of earnings following layoff, discharge, quitting, or other termination of employment;
3) non–job loss—loss of support attributable to change in household composition or the loss of non-earnings income;
4) increased need—budgetary expansion without any change in income or resources, or the occurrence of special need; and
5) miscellaneous—a variety of reasons covering numerous disparate circumstances.

Some caution should be observed in the use of these data, whose reliability is a function of the degree of verification the DOSS has been able to exercise, which has varied from time to time and from center to center, depending primarily upon changing administrative policy. During the late 1960s a policy of eligibility by declaration

31

was introduced, and it remained in force until 1972. At the federal level, the use of Social Security records to substantiate the employment and earnings declarations of welfare applicants and recipients is prohibited. Accordingly, it has been alleged that the frequency of the two major precipitants of dependency, loss of income consequent to unemployment and desertion, is inflated and that the rolls harbor an unknown number of cases of concealed employment and apparent desertion. Quantification of this illicit sector of the caseload can only be the subject of conjecture. Our analysis of the precipitants of dependency was undertaken with this caveat in mind.

Table 3.3 reveals that the largest proportion of males sought welfare following job loss (37 percent). Among females job loss accounts for less than a quarter of the first acceptances. If unemployment for reasons of health and job loss are combined, they account for about two-thirds of all male first acceptances but for only half of those for females. Non-job-related need essentially affected female household heads, for two-fifths of whom it constituted the precipitant for welfare, in contrast with 14 percent of males.

Time, however, has witnessed shifts in the relative importance of the major causes of dependency. Beginning in 1967, health

Table 3.3 Reason for First Acceptance, by Sex of Welfare Recipient and Date of First Acceptance (in percent)

Reason	Date of first acceptance		
	Before 1967	1967–69	1970–71
Males	(121)	(179)	(207)
Health	23	32	31
Job loss	37	29	43
Non-job loss	21	14	11
Increased need	7	7	6
Miscellaneous	12	18	9
Females	(439)	(363)	(215)
Health	24	27	31
Job loss	28	19	21
Non-job loss	36	42	40
Increased need	5	5	4
Miscellaneous	7	6	4

NOTES: Response rate: 90 percent. Figures in parentheses represent absolute numbers.

reasons increased significantly over the earlier period for both males and females, rising to 30 percent of all first acceptances in the latter period. Job loss, on the other hand, which declined markedly as a cause in 1967–69, showed a slight rise among females and a dramatic increase among males during the 1970–71 recession. In the absence of any known change in general health indices during the brief two-year span 1967–69, the increase in initial acceptance for reasons of health suggests that moderately disabling illness that was insufficient in severity or chronicity to satisfy criteria for disability assistance came to be judged an adequate cause for family- or general-assistance acceptance. It might alternatively be hypothesized that individuals who had been accepted in earlier years for reasons of health subsequently either returned to self-support or were transferred to the adult welfare categories, currently the SSI caseload.

First Acceptance and Subsequent Assistance History

Ideally a study of the relationship between employment and dependency should determine the association between the reason for first acceptance and subsequent reliance on public assistance. Specifically it would be desirable to determine whether persons who first seek assistance for employment-related reasons— temporary illness or job loss—are less likely than others to use assistance continuously and for long durations.

However, a study based upon a sample of recipients drawn at a fixed point in time can only provide partial insights into dependency patterns. Any analysis of such recipients in terms of reason for first acceptance must necessarily combine those accepted recently for a given reason with those accepted far earlier for the same reason. Since, as already indicated (table 3.3), the relative frequency of each reason has varied over time, any examination of first-acceptance reasons is biased by the different distributions of acceptance reasons over time. Moreover, as noted earlier, sample members accepted in an earlier time period are representative only of the chronically dependent, not of all those accepted in that period. Only a cohort study of persons first accepted within a fixed time period, and not a sample of cases active at a given point, would permit detailed analysis of patterns of dependency.

Table 3.4 Patterns of Dependency, by Sex of Welfare Recipient and Reason for First Opening (in percent)

Reason	Continuous dependency	Interrupted dependency
Males	(274)	(224)
Health	55	45
Job loss	53	47
Non-job loss	55	45
Increased need	53	47
Miscellaneous	58	42
Females	(662)	(357)
Health	60	40
Job loss	56	44
Non-job loss	73	27
Increased need	71	29
Miscellaneous	57	43

NOTES: Response rate: 90 percent. Figures in parentheses represent absolute numbers.

With these caveats in mind, we may consider the kind of evidence the sample does provide with respect to acceptance reasons and subsequent assistance history. Table 3.4 classifies male and female household heads by reason for first acceptance and indicates whether first acceptance resulted in continuous or interrupted receipt of public assistance. For males there is little variation in pattern of dependency among first-acceptance reasons. For each reason the share of male heads remaining on assistance continuously is somewhat more than one-half. Regardless of the reason for first seeking assistance, approximately 45 percent of the males in the sample were able to become self-supporting for some period of time between their first acceptance and their current period of dependency.[8]

For females who have been continuously dependent there is a wider variation among reasons for first acceptance. Those first seeking assistance for employment-related reasons are least likely to have remained continuously on assistance. Since job-related openings have increased in importance for females in the most recent time period (table 3.3), this finding is unlikely to be biased by differences in dates of acceptance.

That about 45 percent of all those first receiving assistance for job-related reasons have interrupted histories of dependency should not be interpreted as evidence of a substantial work-welfare dynamic among the caseload. In the first place, individuals who were first accepted for employment-related reasons are only a fraction, although a sizable one, of the total sample. More important, additional analysis of those whose first acceptance was for job loss and who experienced one or more periods of self-support reveals that these interruptions were most often the result of factors other than employment and that the return to dependency for a second time did not reflect loss of another job. Specifically, of 498 males with sufficient data for analysis, 184 (37 percent) were first accepted for job loss. Of this group 86—somewhat less than half—were not continuously dependent upon assistance, but only 25 of them (14 percent) were opened on the second occasion for a second job loss. Viewed in terms of the entire male sample, individuals who initially had turned to welfare following job loss but regained self-support for a time constitute 17 percent, and those whose return to welfare was also occasioned by job loss are only 5 percent of the total. It is clear that only a small fraction of all males have alternated between work and welfare. For females the proportions are even smaller: only 23 percent first opened for job loss, 9 percent opened for job loss and were not continually dependent, and 2 percent had two openings for job-loss reasons.

Additional evidence of limited use of welfare as a buffer to unstable employment emerges from a detailed month-by-month analysis of the status of individual members of the sample during the 46 months from January 1968 to November 1971. During this period 31 percent of the females and 72 percent of the males experienced at least one month of employment. For the vast majority of these cases, male and female, employment preceded their first welfare episode in this period, but once they were accepted for public assistance, dependency continued for the remainder of the 46 months. Only 2 percent of the females and 7 percent of the males were employed between two welfare episodes during the 46 months. This group is slightly larger than that identified as experiencing two successive case openings for job-loss reasons because, although they had some work between periods of dependency, job loss was not their exclusive reason for seeking assistance.

Summary

Studies based upon administrative statistics have indicated substantial turnover in the caseload, and these findings have supported inferences of significant work-welfare interaction. Our findings, based upon longitudinal data drawn from case records, do not substantiate these inferences. Much of the turnover evident in program statistics is what has been called "administrative churning" and is unrelated to either need for assistance or labor-force behavior. Once these short-term closings are eliminated, it becomes apparent that most of those accepted for assistance remain on assistance for substantial periods of time. Analysis of case-history data reveals few who move frequently between work and welfare: only 5 percent of the males and 2 percent of the females in our sample had two or more episodes of assistance precipitated for job-loss reasons. Similarly, small percentages had some work experience between welfare episodes, even if loss of work was not the reason they sought assistance.

4.

Current Work Status and Past Work History

In chapter 3 the public assistance history of the welfare sample was summarized and related to selected personal characteristics of the recipients. In this chapter the focus shifts to the work aspect of the work-welfare relationship. The employability of the household heads of the welfare sample is analyzed from two related perspectives: current and previous employment experience.

Current Work Status

Although work and welfare are not mutually exclusive and welfare recipients may have not only an intermittent but even a continuing relationship with the world of work, the use of traditional labor-force categories to describe this relationship seems inappropriate in the case of a general welfare population, not only because the lack of a work-derived income is obviously a chief causal factor for being on welfare but also because the more precise criteria used by Current Population Survey analysts in determining classification into the various labor-force categories presumably result in greater accuracy. Thus, for example, for a person to be counted as unemployed (not working, but looking for work) in the Current Population Survey, he must during the survey week be either waiting to start a new job or to be recalled from layoff or have engaged in the past four weeks in some specific job-seeking activity, such as going to the Employment Service or answering a want ad. In contrast, the criteria used by caseworkers in answering this question were less dependent upon evidence of such concrete job-seeking activity. For these reasons, it seemed advisable to categorize household heads of the welfare sample less formally as (1) working, (2) not working but looking for work, and (3) not working and not looking for work. When the sample groups are distributed on this basis, the degree of reported participation in some work-related activity is, not surprisingly, low: 42 percent of the 520 males, 78 percent of the 268 females with youngest dependent child aged 18, and 87 percent of the 863 all other females were reported to be neither working nor looking for work. However, more than one in five of the men were reported to be working (and receiving supplementary public assistance), as contrasted with about 6 percent of the women.

Personal Characteristics

An analysis of the individuals in each of the three work-status categories by age, sex, ethnicity, marital status, education, number and ages of children, and reported problems likely to impair employability reveals some major differences within the sample groups. Table 4.1 shows that males working or looking for work at the time of the sample selection share certain characteristics. They are predominantly married men with intact families who are in the prime working age group, between the ages of 25 and 44. Aside from an overrepresentation of whites and others among those looking for work and some overrepresentation of Puerto Ricans among those not working, there is little difference in the ethnic composition of those working or looking for work and those not looking for work. As for schooling level, four out of five males, regardless of work status, have no high-school diploma, but contrary to what might be expected, the pattern of educational attainment of those working is closer to that of those not working than of those looking for work. The former two groups contain in fact both the least educated—about half the members of each has no more than an eighth-grade education—and the best educated, with one in five in each group having at least a high-school diploma. These two groups also resemble each other in patterns of accession to the welfare rolls, with about two-thirds first accepted two years or longer before the time of sample selection. Those looking for

Table 4.1 Work Status and Selected Personal Characteristics of Males (in percent)

Personal characteristics	Work status		
	Working (116)	Looking for work (186)	Not looking for work (218)
Age			
18–24	14	17	12
25–34	32	38	24
35–44	30	24	25
Over 44	24	20	39
Marital status			
Never married	5	12	18
Married, spouse present	92	84	68
Married, spouse absent	3	4	14
Ethnic group			
Puerto Rican	47	46	56
Black	32	30	29
White and other	21	24	15
Educational attainment			
Less than high school	55	38	50
Some high school	24	44	28
High-school graduate	20	14	14
Post-high school	1	4	8
Date of first acceptance			
Before 1967	28	22	30
1967–69	36	27	38
1970–71	36	52	32
Incidence of problems[a]			
Physical	7	11	49
Mental	3	10	9
Police record	3	10	5
Family	—	—	4
Other	3	7	5

NOTES: Response rates: 92–100 percent, except for educational attainment, where range is 61–75 percent. Figures in parentheses represent absolute numbers.

[a] Percentages for "incidence of problems" do not add up to 100 because the category "no problems" is not shown.

work, on the other hand, were relatively recent recipients of welfare, with over half accepted in the period 1970–71.

Here the similarities between men who are working and men who are neither working nor looking for work end. The latter tend to be older—almost 40 percent are over 45, Puerto Rican, and less likely to be living with their wives. Men not looking for work also have a strikingly higher rate of reported physical illness: nearly half were reported by the caseworker as having some health problem, as compared with 7 percent of those working and 11 percent of those looking for work. Among those looking for work, however, the incidence of mental problems is about the same as that of those not working, and the incidence of police records is actually double.

Analysis of the current work status of female household heads with youngest dependent child aged 18 reveals that more than 3 in 4 are neither working nor looking for work. Comparisons among the three types of current work status are thus limited by the small numbers in the group who are working (22) or looking for work (37) (see table 4.2). Within these limitations, some gross differences in age and ethnic distribution are apparent. Those working or looking for work are younger—more than half are under age 45—and more likely to be black, while those not looking for work are older—more than two-thirds are over age 45—and more likely to be Puerto Rican. The former also arrive later on the public assistance rolls. Finally, the proportion of women with reported physical problems who are neither working nor looking for work is high (42 percent), both absolutely and relative to the incidence of such problems reported for women in the other two categories.

Among "all other females" ethnic differences among work-status categories are conspicuous (see table 4.3). Nine out of ten women who are working and over half of those looking for work are black, as compared with two-fifths of those who are not looking for work. In contrast, none among the currently working and only one in four of those looking for work are Puerto Rican, while their proportion of those not seeking work is higher than their sample share. For the women in the sample, educational levels are related to work status: as is true of the general female population, women who are working tend to have more schooling than those who are not. More than one in two of the working women within the "all other female" group have at least a high-school diploma, compared with one in four of those looking for work and one in five of those neither working nor looking for work.

Reported problems are markedly higher for those not looking for work: one-fifth of these women were reported to have physical

Table 4.2   Work Status and Selected Personal Characteristics of Females with Youngest Dependent Child Aged Eighteen (in percent)

	Work status		
Personal characteristics	Working (22)	Looking for work (37)	Not looking for work (209)
Age			
18–24	—	—	—
25–34	5	—	3
35–44	50	51	30
44 and over	45	49	67
Marital status			
Never married	27	19	15
Married, spouse present	14	8	10
Married, spouse absent	59	73	75
Ethnic group			
Puerto Rican	16	50	47
Black	63	39	29
White and other	21	12	24
Educational attainment			
Less than high school	35	73	61
Some high school	41	27	27
High-school graduate	18	—	10
Post-high school	6	—	2
Date of first acceptance			
Before 1967	33	42	68
1967–69	38	25	25
1970–71	29	33	7
Incidence of problems[a]			
Physical	18	11	42
Mental	—	—	1
Police record	—	—	1
Family	4	3	8
Other	—	—	2

NOTES: Response rates: 86–100 percent, except for educational attainment, where range is 56–77 percent. Figures in parentheses represent absolute numbers.

[a] Percentages for "incidence of problems" do not add up to 100 because the category "no problems" is not shown.

problems of varying degrees of severity—a figure almost double that for women working or looking for work but considerably lower than that for males not looking for work. Another fifth of the women not looking for work were reported to have some type of family-related problem. The relation between date of first wel-

41

Table 4.3   Work Status and Selected Personal Characteristics of All Other Females (in percent)

Personal characteristics	Work status		
	Working (52)	Looking for work (58)	Not looking for work (757)
Age			
18–24	12	10	15
25–34	35	19	32
35–44	39	19	25
44 and over	15	52	28
Marital status			
Never married	31	26	24
Married, spouse present	8	9	12
Married, spouse absent	61	66	63
Ethnic group			
Puerto Rican	—	25	39
Black	89	52	40
White	9	14	15
Other	2	9	6
Educational attainment			
Less than high school	14	40	41
Some high school	30	33	39
High-school graduate	38	24	17
Post-high school	19	2	4
Date of first acceptance			
Before 1967	52	26	43
1967–69	36	28	36
1970–71	12	46	21
Incidence of problems[a]			
Physical	12	10	21
Mental	—	5	6
Police record	—	2	1
Family	4	3	21
Other	—	9	2

NOTES: Response rates: 88–100 percent, except for educational attainment, where the range is 68–72 percent. Figures in parentheses represent absolute numbers.

[a] Percentages for "incidence of problems" do not add up to 100 because the category "no problems" is not shown.

fare acceptance and current work status is similar to that for males: the bulk of those looking for work in each case came on the assistance rolls in 1970–71, while both those currently working and those neither working nor looking for work are more likely to be longer-term recipients of public assistance.

Since "all other females" are usually heads of one-parent households, the employment potential of these women is conditioned by childcare responsibilities, making it important to consider in some detail both the number and ages of their children. The majority of those looking for work had no children at home, compared with less than one-fifth of those currently working and of those neither working nor looking for work.

Not surprisingly, the children of working mothers are more likely to be of school age than of pre-school age, in contrast to children of women not looking for work. Moreover, the latter are most likely to have large families of three or more children, including some under six; 28 percent fit this description, compared with only 10 percent of those currently working. Nonetheless, it is clear that a substantial portion of those neither working nor looking for work have limited childcare responsibilities; two-fifths have either no children or only one or two children of school age.

How employable are the women who no longer have dependent children at home? They are in the oldest age group, with 70 percent over 45, and, like other females in the sample in the same age group, poorly educated, with three out of four having less than a high-school diploma. Nearly two-thirds were reported as having some special problem, half of them physical in nature. A majority have had some work experience, but another two-fifths have never worked. Thus the overall picture of nonworking female household heads with no dependent children is one of minimally educated, older women beset with physical and other problems and often without any previous work experience. Since more than half of "all other females" who were reported to be looking for work belong to this subset, there is some question as to the realism of the response which led the caseworker to assign them to this work-status category.

On the other hand, analysis of the 757 "all other females" who are neither working nor looking for work—the largest subgroup within the whole sample—revealed that one in five possessed characteristics which, taken together, indicated the presence of some employment potential. These were women who were between the ages of 18 and 44, who had some high-school education, and who, while currently not working, had had some previous work experience. Seventy percent had jobs which had terminated sometime in the four-year period preceding sample selection; another 20 percent had been out of the labor market for five to ten years. Over three-quarters had no reported problems, and the problems reported for the rest concerned about equally physical conditions and childcare responsibilities. Eleven percent had no children present in the household, and another 29 percent had no children under 6 years of age. The remaining 60 percent had some pre-schoolers at home. A sizable number of these 149 women might reasonably be considered employable if childcare arrangements were made available for those who require them.

An indication of the yearly gross income they could earn from full-time employment is provided by 1970 census earnings data for the female experienced civilian labor force.[1] For black women, median earnings ranged from $5,567 for clerical jobs to $3,124 for domestic work; they were somewhat lower for Puerto Rican women in each occupational category. Since under AFDC rules an AFDC mother who obtains employment is entitled to deduct the first $30 of monthly wages plus one-third of the balance in calculating her grant, she is assured a net gain for each increase in income earned, since her eligibility for (some) public assistance, food stamps, free school lunches, housing subsidies (over and above rent payments), medical assistance, and day care is maintained up to an earned income of $9,000. Thus an AFDC mother with two school-age children and one preschooler requiring day care (a situation descriptive of perhaps 60 percent of the potential employables discussed above) who obtained employment at $5,000 per year would, because of the income-disregard feature, still be entitled to a hypothetical maximum of over $6,600 in benefits,[2] in addition to her disposable income of $4,000. If, however, benefits are restricted to those which are usually available (food stamps, free school lunches, and medical assistance), a more realistic benefits package would come to $3,244, making for a combined cash and in-kind income of $7,246, or $35 more per week than the value of the total package of benefits that would be provided if she did not work.

Employment History

An analysis of the personal characteristics and current work status of the three sample groups provides only a partial basis for an assessment of the potential employability of the members of these groups. Also important for such an assessment was an analysis of the actual past employment experience of the individuals involved, which involved identifying for each sample group the share of those looking for work and the share of those not looking for work who have past employment experience. For virtually all of the males and almost three in four of the females—80 percent of all household heads—affirmative answers were given to the question, Ever Worked? Detailed information was also required on the last job before the first public assistance episode and on all jobs held since 1968; because of the large proportion of the total sample first accepted after 1968, the major part of actual job experience is assumed to have been included. The responses revealed considerable variability in the reported work, ranging from a total of two weeks of informal baby-sitting to many years of steady employment. Two minimal criteria were imposed therefore to determine what could realistically be counted as work experience: a total work experience in all jobs held of at least three months and the provision of some documentation of reported employment (information on industry, occupation, wages, and so on). On this basis 63 percent of the total sample—83 percent of the men and 54 percent of the women—were found to have what is called in this study an "effective" work history. The use of these criteria has led to some degree of underestimation of work experience.

The major finding is that half of the 929 females not looking for work have no effective work history. The much smaller number of women who are looking for work (92) are more likely to have had previous employment, but over one-third of "all other females" in this category had no effective work history. While the vast majority of men who are looking for work had previous "effective" work experience, more than one-quarter of the larger number not seeking work had none.

Among the substantial number of nonworking household heads

45

who lack an effective work history, ethnicity produces some variability (see table 4.4). The underrepresentation of Puerto Rican women among those currently working or looking for work is duplicated in their work histories; they are less likely to have an effective work history, especially in contrast to black women, three out of five of whom have work experience. There is far less variation among males by ethnic group, confirming national findings that cultural factors are operative in limiting the employment of Puerto Rican women.[3]

Age is also a differentiating factor in the work histories of non-working males and females. For both sexes the youngest public-assistance recipients, ages 18 to 24, are least likely to have an effective work history, while those from 35 to 44 are more likely to have one. The most important finding, however, is an absence of effective work histories for approximately half of all nonworking females and for a sizable fraction, ranging from one-fifth to one-third, of nonworking males in each age group.

For those individuals with a past work history it is possible to assess further the quality of this experience by examining its duration. Indirect evidence is derived from information on the receipt of unemployment insurance benefits (UIB), since eligibility for these benefits requires a specific minimum duration of covered employment. Between 1968 and 1971 such benefits were received

Table 4.4 Work History of Household Heads Not Working, by Ethnic Group (in percent)

| Work history | Ethnic group | | |
	Black	Puerto Rican	White and other
Males	(128)	(214)	(84)
Effective work history	81	76	75
No effective work history	19	24	25
Females with youngest dependent child aged 18	(65)	(103)	(48)
Effective work history	63	51	52
No effective work history	37	49	48
All other females	(322)	(278)	(158)
Effective work history	59	38	51
No effective work history	41	62	49

NOTE: Figures in parentheses represent absolute numbers.

by a total of 89 males and 30 females, or 20 percent of the males and 5 percent of the females, who were either currently working in 1971 or who were not currently working but had an effective employment history in the past.

Limited direct evidence on the total work duration of the household heads can be obtained from the collected data, which reveal relatively brief work histories even when age is taken into account. If "short duration" is defined as under one year for those aged 18 to 24, under two years for those 25 to 34, and under three years for all others, then nearly half of the nonworking males and more than half of the nonworking females have relatively short work histories.

A further analysis was made of the work duration of the 751 household heads who had been employed at least one month in the 46-month period between January 1968 and the date of sample drawing, a period for which information was relatively complete.[4] As indicated in chapter 3, almost three-quarters of the men and somewhat less than one-third of the women had worked during this period or had had a combination of work and welfare or work and unemployment insurance benefits. Table 4.5 shows that work duration is related to age and sex, increasing generally with age and usually lower for women than for men at all ages. In total, almost two in five had worked less than one year, and three in five less than two years, although this period was largely dominated by boom conditions. Workers over the age of 35 had the longest work durations; included in this group, however, are the currently em-

Table 4.5   Number of Months Worked between January 1968 and October 1971, by Sex and Age of Jobholder (in percent)

	Age of jobholder							
	Males				Females			
Number of months worked	18–24 (66)	25–34 (138)	35–44 (96)	over 44 (98)	18–24 (63)	25–34 (100)	35–44 (97)	over 44 (95)
1–5	36	17	7	12	41	15	17	20
6–11	15	16	12	11	16	28	27	14
12–23	26	27	27	28	30	25	19	27
24–35	20	25	25	30	10	19	16	19
36–46	3	15	29	19	3	13	21	20

NOTE: Figures in parentheses represent absolute numbers.

ployed who have distinctly longer work durations than other members of the sample. Men over the age of 45 exhibit a decline in work duration that conforms to national trends for men in this age group. Parenthetically, it should be noted that work precedes welfare in almost all cases and that virtually no cases of reemployment after welfare acceptance were reported.

Additional light is shed on the nature of the work experience by data on union membership, which is usually equated with increased job security and regularity of employment. The degree of such membership was minimal: fewer than 10 percent had belonged to a union in the past, and 5 percent still retained membership at the time of the survey. This small number was distributed among several unions, with the largest number of memberships recorded for the International Ladies Garment Workers' Union and the Hotel and Restaurant Employee's Union.

An indicator of possible upgrading and increased employment potential is provided by information on participation in training programs. Ten percent had had some vocational training, and another 13 percent had participated in public training programs such as WIN, MDTA, HARYOU, and Job Corps. Of the 8 percent who had participated in the WIN program, two-thirds were currently enrolled, one quarter had dropped out, and fewer than 10 percent had completed the program.

Thus far we have examined the work experience of household heads only. However, since the presence of additional workers in a family is often critical to their capacity for self-support, it is useful to consider the work experience of other household members. In chapter 2 it was noted that 79 percent of the male household heads and 11 percent and 12 percent, respectively, of the two female groups had a spouse present. Analysis of the work experience of the spouses revealed that only 18 percent of the wives of male household heads and 25 percent of the husbands of female household heads had worked at any time. Most of their work experience was in the past; only 5 percent of all spouses are currently working, with another 5 percent looking for work. Given the varying accounts of unreported and illicit employment among public assistance populations and the limited degree of surveillance that the DOSS is able to exercise, these work figures should be viewed as suggestive but not definitive.

Other family members who may have employment experience are teenage dependent children. However, since DOSS regulations do not require that income from their employment be reported, such employment is generally not described in the case record and is therefore not reported in the study questionnaire. Consequently, no assessment of the employment experience of teenage children has been attempted.

Summary

Analysis of the work status and work history of the welfare sample groups yields several important findings. First, despite the availability of supplementation for Home Relief recipients and of work incentives for AFDC mothers, work participation rates are strikingly low. Further, a substantial share of all welfare recipients (one-quarter of the males, half the females whose youngest dependent child is 18, and more than half of "all other" females) who are neither working nor looking for work had no effective past work history. Second, ethnicity is a differentiating factor among women, with Puerto Ricans not represented at all among the currently working and overrepresented among those neither working nor looking for work, while the reverse applies to black women. Third, although education is not related to work status among males, among females the better-educated are more likely to be working. Fourth, age is responsible for some further degree of variability, especially for males. Older males comprise a disproportionate share of those neither working nor looking for work. Among females, in contrast, those reported to be looking for work are largely in the prime age groups. However, many of the women who lack childcare responsibilities, either because their youngest child is 18 or because they have no dependent children, but are neither working nor looking for work have additional characteristics that impair their employability. These women are older, have a limited education, and have a high incidence of reported problems.

5

The Nature of the Jobs

In the previous chapter the general dimensions of the employment status and experience of the welfare sample were established. In this chapter the nature of the jobs in which this population secures employment is analyzed. All jobs held by the group since 1968 and the last job held before the first public assistance episode are examined in terms of occupation and industry, wage rate, duration, and reasons for termination.[1] Further subdivision of work experience into three broad time periods permits identification of significant shifts in these characteristics over time.

It should be emphasized that the data in this chapter refer to jobs, not to individuals. If a single individual has had severaj jobs, each of these jobs is counted separately; an individual without any employment experience is excluded from the data base. The focus is on the type of jobs held by those welfare recipients who have worked.

The New York City Labor Market

The dominance of migrants in the welfare sample, 85 percent of whom were over the age of 18 when they arrived, suggests the inclusion of some jobs preceding migration into the city. However, the large majority of the reported jobs are in New York City, and meaningful analysis and realistic policy measures must be related to the characteristics of and trends in the city's labor market. From the viewpoint of job analysis the following are among the more significant:

1. Within 3.5 million jobs (exclusive of self-employment), New York has the largest and most diversified labor market of any city in the country.

2. Since 1960 the growing sectors of the city's economy have been finance, insurance, and real estate (FIRE); services, particularly health; and state and local government. The declining sectors have been manufacturing (led by the apparel industry), wholesale and retail trade, construction, transportation, and public utilities. New York City now has a "high service" economy, with almost 80 percent of its total work force employed by relatively small firms in the non-goods-producing sector. In spite of the rapid growth in government employment, about six out of every seven workers are employed in the private sector.[2]

3. This combination of trends has resulted in a predominantly white-collar occupational structure; in 1970 almost 60 percent of the work force was distributed among such white-collar categories as professional and technical workers, managers, and clerical and sales workers. Fewer than 30 percent were blue-collar and unskilled workers; the rest were service workers. This trend was particularly pronounced for women, 70 percent of whom were in white-collar jobs, compared with 50 percent of the men.

4. Blacks and Puerto Ricans participated in these occupational shifts to a limited degree. Blue-collar jobs remained the most important occupational category for minority men, although one-third of the black men and 27 percent of the Puerto Rican men had white-collar jobs. For the women, white-collar jobs became the major category; more than half the black women and almost half the Puerto Rican women had such jobs. In spite of these shifts, however, unemployment rates among minority groups were higher, and median incomes were lower, than those for whites.[3]

5. New York has an abundance of both high- and low-wage jobs The median weekly earnings for all workers in 1969 was $129, and for full-time workers it was $141.[4]

6. Its heterogeneous industry mix has until recently served to insulate the New York job market from the more extreme swings in the business cycle. The recession of 1970–71, how-

ever, combined with the secular decline in several industries, led to a New York City unemployment rate that was higher than the national rate and the loss of over a quarter of a million jobs between 1969 and 1972, which effectively eliminated the large employment gains of the 1960s.[5]

Characteristics of Past Jobs

The jobs held by welfare recipients may be described in terms of their industrial and occupational characteristics. While some analysts select either occupation or industry as a basis for describing employment, a combination of both provides a more accurate picture of particular jobs and may be developed through the use of a matrix composed of five broad occupational classifications (white-collar, blue-collar, unskilled labor, domestic service, and other services) and nine industrial categories (apparel manufacturing, all other manufacturing, utilities including transportation and communication, business and professional services, retail and wholesale trade, restaurants and hotels, personal and health services, government, and all others). While the matrix provides 45 possible occupation-industry cells, it was found that 16 accounted for the majority of jobs held by the welfare sample. These 16 cells, together with a residual "all others" industry category for each occupational group, provide the basis for much of the analysis in this chapter.

Analysis of the occupation-industry distribution of jobs held by males and females during three time periods—before 1968, 1968–69, and 1970–71—and terminating in those periods revealed some major shifts over time for males and females alike. For both sexes blue-collar jobs, although declining relatively, were most importnt in each time period and even in 1970–71 provided jobs for two out of every five men and one in every three women. Unskilled labor and other services each provided approximately 20–25 percent of all male jobs and 10–15 percent of all female jobs in every period. Domestic service was important only for females and consistently provided one-fifth of all female jobs in each period.

Reflecting the general occupational shift in the New York City labor market, the greatest change took place in white-collar employment, where the growth of jobs was rapid. The proportion of white-collar female jobs increased from one in seven to one in four; for males the large increase took place at the end of the period, when white-collar jobs rose to almost one-quarter of the total. By 1970–71 white-collar jobs were the second most important category for females and males alike.

An analysis of past jobs by the ethnicity as well as the sex of the jobholder reveals little difference among males in the occupation-industry distribution of jobs held in each time period (table 5.1) but important differences among females (table 5.2).[6] The major finding is a shift among black women away from blue-collar jobs in manufacturing and domestic work toward white-collar jobs in business services, trade, and utilities. There was no such dramatic change for Puerto Rican women, who had, however, moved out of services into unskilled and blue-collar jobs in (nonapparel) manufacturing and had secured a modest number of white-collar jobs. The number of jobs held by white females in the most recent period is too small to permit an analysis of trends. Overall, the sex-ethnic data indicate that the shift to white-collar employment among females is most marked among blacks. Jobs may be described in terms of their wage level, as well as in terms of their occupation-industry characteristics.[7] In order to compare wage levels of different time periods, the reported current weekly wage rates of each job were converted to constant (1967) dollar values. The findings indicate that both male and female wage levels have been rising but that females consistently have held jobs paying less than jobs held by males. In 1970–71 almost half the jobs held by women were in the $61–$80 range; more than half of the jobs held by males paid over $80 per week, compared with less than one in five of those held by females.[8] Each of these figures, however, represents a marked increase in the share of jobs paying over $80 when compared with the number in the period before 1969. For females, the proportion had almost doubled; for males there had been a 38 percent rise.

For the period 1969–71 occupation-industry information was combined with earnings data to permit identification of those areas which account for higher- and lower-wage jobs. Among the jobs held by males, blue-collar work accounts for the largest share at all

Table 5.1 Occupation-Industry Distribution of Past Jobs of Males, by Ethnic Group and Period of Job Termination (in percent)

	Period of job termination								
	Blacks			Puerto Ricans			Whites		
Occupation-industry category	Before 1968 (27)	1968-69 (24)	1970-71 (33)	Before 1968 (37)	1968-69 (32)	1970-71 (64)	Before 1968 (13)	1968-69 (9)	1970-71 (24)
White-collar									
Business and professional	—	—	12	—	—	3	—	—	13
Trade	—	—	6	—	3	6	15	—	8
Utilities	—	8	—	—	—	—	—	—	4
Personal and health services	—	—	—	—	—	—	—	11	—
All other	—	4	3	5	3	10	15	—	8
Total white-collar	—	12	21	5	6	19	31	11	33
Blue-collar									
Apparel manufacture	4	4	3	3	3	3	—	—	—
Other manufactures	15	21	12	35	13	25	15	22	21
Utilities	4	4	6	—	3	—	23	22	4
Trade	11	8	3	—	3	2	—	—	4
All others	14	13	9	—	9	11	15	34	4
Total blue-collar	48	50	33	38	31	41	54	78	33

Other services

Restaurant and hotel	4	4	9	—	11	13	3	7	—	—
Personal and health	4	4	—	3	3	6	3	—	—	—
Business and professional	14	13	3	3	3	13	3	—	11	13
Government	4	4	6	—	2	—	5	—	—	—
All other	11	—	3	3	2	—	3	—	—	4
Total other services	37	25	21	19	31	17	7	—	11	17

Unskilled labor

Apparel manufacture	—	—	—	3	6	5	7	—	—	—
Other manufactures	8	—	6	22	19	6	3	—	—	9
Trade	—	—	3	2	3	3	3	—	—	—
All other	7	13	15	11	3	3	9	—	—	8
Total unskilled labor	15	13	24	38	31	23	7	—	—	17

NOTES: Figures in parentheses represent absolute numbers. Totals may not add to 100 percent because of rounding.

Table 5.2 Occupation-Industry Distribution of Past Jobs of Females, by Ethnic Group and Period of Job Termination (in percent)

	Period of job termination								
	Blacks			Puerto Ricans			Whites		
Occupation-industry category	Before 1968 (133)	1968–69 (39)	1970–71 (30)	Before 1968 (84)	1968–69 (31)	1970–71 (21)	Before 1968 (30)	1968–69 (19)	1970–71 (8)
White-collar									
Business and professional	4	8	10	—	3	5	21	5	12
Trade	4	10	10	9	—	—	—	5	12
Utilities	1	—	7	1	3	—	8	—	—
Personal and health services	2	—	3	—	3	—	—	5	12
All other	1	5	3	—	6	10	5	5	25
Total white-collar	12	23	33	10	16	14	34	21	62
Blue-collar									
Apparel manufacture	8	3	3	28	16	14	10	10	12
Other manufactures	16	13	7	19	26	24	21	16	—
Utilities	—	—	—	—	—	—	—	—	—
Trade	1	—	—	—	—	—	3	—	—
All others	4	2	7	4	—	10	3	—	25
Total blue-collar	29	18	17	51	42	48	37	26	38

Domestic service	36	41	27	13	16	10	—	5	—
Other services									
Restaurant and hotel	6	8	3	5	6	—	10	21	—
Personal and health	7	2	13	5	—	—	5	10	—
Business and professional	—	—	3	1	—	—	—	—	—
Government	—	—	—	1	—	—	—	5	—
All other	2	—	—	1	3	—	8	—	—
Total other services	15	10	20	13	10	—	24	37	—
Unskilled labor									
Apparel manufacture	2	—	—	6	3	10	3	5	—
Other manufactures	5	3	—	7	10	14	3	—	—
Trade	—	3	—	—	—	—	—	—	—
All other	1	2	3	—	3	5	—	5	—
Total unskilled labor	8	8	3	13	16	29	5	10	—

NOTES: Figures in parentheses represent absolute numbers. Totals may not add to 100 percent because of rounding.

wage levels, but the figure dips from 50 percent of those earning between $41 and $60 to 35 percent of those earning over $80. At this highest wage level, however, white-collar jobs are a quarter of the male total; white-collar jobs were not found at the lowest wage level and constituted only 8 percent of those jobs paying between $41 and $60.

Among the jobs held by females, domestic work accounts for over half of the jobs paying under $40 weekly but for only 5 percent of those at the highest level. Many of these are, however, part-time and include unspecified in-kind payments. In contrast, white-collar work accounts for over half of the highest-wage jobs and for only 7 percent of those in the lowest-wage category. Almost half of all the blue-collar jobs held by women paid between $61 and $80, and the rest were fairly evenly distributed between higher- and lower-wage levels.

In addition to wages, another important characteristic of jobs is their stability. An analysis of the duration of jobs held by male and female recipients that were terminated between 1968 and 1971 indicates that two-fifths of all these jobs were of short duration (that is, less than one year) and that approximately one-fifth lasted five years or longer. Most short-duration jobs were white-collar, reflecting in part the fact that the shift to such employment came late in the period. White-collar jobs in professional and business services were tied with service work in restaurants and hotels as the specific occupation-industry category with the highest proportion (56 percent) of short-duration jobs. Domestic work had the largest share (39 percent) of jobs lasting over five years, followed by blue-collar work (26 percent).

The duration of past jobs held by public assistance recipients is a function of the type of work, which may be short-lived or intermittent, and of the personal circumstances of the individuals, which may cause them to leave their jobs. When the jobs terminated between 1968 and 1971 are classified by reasons for termination, poor health is by far the most important reported reason, accounting for two-fifths of all job terminations, almost one-half of those in the 1968–69 boom period and over one-third during the recession of 1970–71. Over one-fifth of the jobs were terminated because of lay-offs and 17 percent because of discharges. Not surprisingly, these latter figures were higher (27 percent and 19 percent, respectively) during the recession period than during the more prosperous years of 1968 and 1969. The importance of lay-offs and firings as reasons for termination varies widely, but since no sharp distinctions can be drawn between them, only limited conclusions can emerge from their differential distribution. Hardly any of the domestic jobs ended because of a layoff, in contrast to three-quarters of the unskilled jobs in the apparel industry and over a third of the more skilled blue-collar jobs in the same industry. Discharges were least common in domestic work and tended to be highest in white-collar fields. Quitting and personal reasons, which accounted for the termination of one in five jobs held between 1968 and 1971, were highest in the white-collar category. The propor-tion remained the same even with the downturn in the economy, reflecting perhaps the increased resort to public assistance.

In sum, this analysis of the past jobs held by current public assistance recipients yields several important findings. The distri-bution of the jobs in which these individuals have worked reflects some of the changes in the New York economy; illustratively, about one-quarter of the jobs held by sample members during 1970–71 were white-collar—more than triple the number in the pre-1968 period. White-collar jobs held by women were more numerous than domestic jobs—a reversal of the pre-1968 situa-tion. The changing occupation-industry mix of jobs was reflected in their wage levels. By 1970–71 over 55 percent of the jobs held by males paid a weekly wage of over $80, equivalent to a current (June 1974) dollar figure of over $123. However, only 17 percent of the jobs held by females paid at least this much. Finally, the duration of jobs held by both males and females was relatively short, with 43 percent lasting less than one year and 59 percent less than two years, but these brief durations may have been a function of the recession of 1970–1971 rather than of the nature of the jobs. Only an upturn in the economy could establish the degree of basic change in the job market for this population.

Jobs of the Currently Employed

As noted in chapter 4, approximately 22 percent of the males and 7 percent of the females in the sample were currently employed. The jobs held by this group were compared with jobs terminated in the most recent period, 1970–71.

Among males, the continuing jobs are more heavily concentrated in the blue-collar and other-services categories and are less likely to be in white-collar fields. For currently working women who are primarily black a different job picture emerges: jobs held by them conform more closely to shifts in the New York City economy out of apparel and other manufactures to white-collar and other service employment. Within the other-services category women are presently concentrated in health services, and within the white-collar category, in the public sector.

Further analysis shows that the occupation and industry distributions of current jobs differ according to age for both males and females. Among men the largest concentration of jobs are blue-collar non-apparel-manufacturing jobs at every age level except between 25 and 34 years; for this group restaurant and hotel and health jobs are dominant. Representation of younger women (below 35) in white-collar jobs is high but diminishes with age. Older women tend to be employed as domestics and in other services. The occupation-industry distribution of currently employed women thus largely reflects the general shifts in black female employment previously described.

The wage rates for current jobs present a more favorable picture than those of recently terminated jobs: more than nine out of ten of the currently employed males held jobs that paid more than $80 a week (in 1967 dollars) only 55 percent of the recently terminated jobs paid as much. The difference is more striking among women; seven out of ten of the current jobs were in the highest pay range, compared with 17 percent of the recently terminated jobs.

The jobs held by the currently employed are also of longer duration than those recently terminated. More than two-fifths of the latter had a duration of less than one year, but only a quarter of the currently employed have held their present job for so short a period. Moreover, the currently employed have longer total work histories than do welfare recipients who are not presently employed. More than two out of five currently employed males and females have total work histories of more than five years, compared with one out of four nonemployed males, and one out of five nonemployed females, with past work experience.

These descriptive job data together with the information on personal characteristics presented in chapter 4 indicate that the currently employed are a distinct subset of the general welfare population. They are primarily males; although men are only a third of the total sample, they are three-fifths of the currently employed. More than nine out of ten of these currently employed men are heads of intact households, and they tend to be of prime working age. Although the vast majority (79 percent) lack a high-school diploma, most of them have secured jobs in the service and manufacturing sectors of the local economy and earn wages that exceed $120 in current dollar terms. Since these jobs are relatively stable, these men have accumulated substantial work experience.

Why do these men require public assistance? The answer is generally that their earnings are inadequate even by welfare standards to support their large families. Nearly three-quarters of currently employed males have at least five persons in their households, and more than one-third have households of seven or more persons.

The family situation of currently employed men is illustrated by these comments appended to the questionnaires by caseworkers.

1. Mr. W has a very good work history. He is currently receiving public assistance because the income from employment is not sufficient to meet the needs of his 9 (nine) member family.
2. This legally married couple has 3 children, and they are expecting a 4th child. His wages are not adequate for the family, and the family is being supplemented by the Dept.
3. The primary problems is that Mr. D's income does not meet his family's needs and Mr. D is aware that due to lack of ed-[ucation] and a language barrier, he will never earn sufficient money to care for his family without public asistance. This has never been a deterrent in his obtaining work on a somewhat steady basis. Mrs. D does not speak English well, but she is friendly. She is a good homemaker. The children are well reared and have good attendance in school.

6

Follow-up: Welfare Experience of the Sample,

January 1972–May 1973

To complement the retrospective survey of the sample, cohort analysis was undertaken on the basis of data derived from the H-DRAT file (Historic-Daily Record of Actions Taken), an ongoing data base that has been maintained by the New York City DOSS since January 1972. This file contains a chronological record of specified significant actions undergone by every case on the assistance rolls. Since each case is distinguished by a specific number assigned to it at the time of initial opening, it is now possible to reconstruct individual case histories from ongoing computerized data.

The types of action recorded on the file of significance to this study are openings, reopenings, closings, and category change, each with its date of occurrence and, in the case of (re)openings and closings, the official coded reason.

The usefulness of the file is somewhat limited by its recency; information prior to 1972 can be retrieved only via laborious case-record search. For this study, however, which has gathered comprehensive historic data for the sample prior to November 1971, the H-DRAT file provided a unique opportunity to track each case over a defined forward period, January 1972–May 1973, and to link observed patterns of activity to demographic characteristics and to selected aspects of welfare history and employment that had been defined through analysis of the original questionnaire-elicited data. The objective was to isolate the dimensions and the determinants of welfare mobility, with specific attention to the alternative of self-support via employment. One specific research question illuminated by the availability of follow-up data was the outcome of AFDC eligibility expiration for mothers whose youngest child outgrew dependency status upon reaching the age of 18. Are such recipients absorbed into the labor force, or is dependence maintained through transfer to another assistance category?

Preliminary matching of the sample with the DOSS check-issuing file revealed that as of July 1973, 75 percent of the original survey cases were on the welfare rolls. This should not imply that all but 25 percent of cases active in September 1971 had received welfare uninterruptedly for the succeeding 21 months. Almost 60 percent were found to be represented on the H-DRAT file, with a median of one action per case, although the range is as high as seven. Distribution of actions by type, however, indicates that almost 50 percent of these reflect administrative change rather than any actual shift in dependency status. By following the convention adopted in the analysis of the earlier welfare history of disregarding erroneous closings and very brief intervals between successive episodes of dependency, the frequency of events describing true welfare mobility is further reduced. This distribution is, however, suggestive at best, since it relates to actions rather than to individuals. In order to distinguish among members of the sample by degree of actual mobility during the 17-month period under examination, each case was scrutinized for closings, openings, and reopenings. Within this definitional framework, slightly over 30 percent of all the cases in the sample were found to have undergone some alteration in welfare status during the period November 1971–May 1973.

A useful approach to differential utilization of public assistance might distinguish among continuing dependents who, once accepted, persist as the stable core of the caseload; one-time recipients who are supported by welfare for a defined period and then return to self-support; and intermittent welfare enrollees, who receive assistance episodically. Since the seventeen-month span of the H-DRAT file is insufficient for a meaningful tripartite division of this sort, the analysis proceeded from a distribution of the sample between cases that had experienced at least one closing and those that had remained continuously on assistance. It should be noted that welfare continuity refers only to the episode of dependency in effect at the time of the study, November 1971, and does not extend to prior assistance history. Thus an individual who had experienced multiple earlier periods of dependency might be classified as a continuous beneficiary in the analysis of the H-DRAT follow-up data.[1]

Cases that had undergone no action other than recategorization, which in terms of welfare mobility are included within the group of continuing recipients, were nevertheless isolated as a means of tracing the progress of AFDC mothers whose youngest dependent child was approaching the mandatory termination age of 18. As a first approximation toward elucidating specific characteristics of intermittent public assistance beneficiaries, a subset of all cases that were terminated during the first five months of the follow-up period was traced for welfare activity during the succeeding year, and these were classified as having remained closed or having returned to the public assistance rolls by the end of the period.

Distribution of the sample caseload among these various utilization categories was analyzed by demographic characteristics and related to the duration of the most recent episode of public assistance. Reasons for welfare termination during the seventeen-month follow-up period were similarly examined and compared with earlier termination reasons. In the light of the specific focus of the study upon the relationship between dependency and employment experience, the group that was terminated due to employment or increased earnings was subjected to closer scrutiny.

Public Assistance Experience of the Sample,
November 1971–May 1973

While the great majority of the welfare sample (68 percent) remained uninterruptedly on assistance throughout the final two months of 1971 and the follow-up period, January 1972–mid-May 1973, 32 percent had undergone at least one closing; of the latter, approximately one-third had reopened before the end of the period. Given sample stratification, it is significant that in each of the component subpopulations—male household heads, female AFDC recipients with a single dependent child approaching 18, and all other female household heads—continuous dependency was the rule for the majority of cases, although the proportion ranged from a low of 60 percent for males to almost 75 percent for "all other" females (table 6.1). Within these differentially defined populations age accounted for further variability, with the lowest rates of continuous dependency found among the youngest recipients, 18 to 24 years old, an age group which, for obvious reasons, includes only males and "all other" females. The youngest group of mothers of 18-year-old dependents, women in the mid-thirties, also shows a low proportion of continuous dependency, although they are numerically few. Among males, continuous dependency rates vary directly with age; among females they peak in the middle years and show some slackening in the oldest age category, particularly where only a single dependent child remains. Not unexpectedly, the most persistent group of welfare recipients are

Table 6.1 Public Assistance Status of Sample Groups in Follow-up Period January 1972–May 1973 (in percent)

| Sample group | Public assistance status | | |
| | Continuous | Closed | |
		Reopened	Not reopened
Males			
18–24	46	18	36
25–34	59	14	27
35–44	64	15	20
Over 44	65	11	24
Percentage of total	*60*	*14*	*26*
Females with youngest dependent child aged 18[a]			
18–24	—	—	—
25–34	43	14	43
35–44	70	5	25
Over 44	65	9	26
Percentage of total	*66*	*8*	*26*
All other females			
18–24	65	10	25
25–34	78	6	16
35–44	71	12	18
Over 44	75	10	16
Percentage of total	*73*	*9*	*18*

[a] Among the females with a youngest dependent child aged 18 who are classified as continuously receiving assistance 72 were reclassified from AFDC to some other category. They are distributed among the age categories as follows: ages 35 to 44—42 percent; over 44—58 percent.

females aged 25 to 34, for whom presumably childcare responsibilities are at their peak.

AFDC mothers with a single dependent child aged 18, particularly those 45 years and over, were the most likely group to have been reclassified (an action included under continuous receipt of public assistance). Compared with a reclassification rate of 14 percent for the men and 12 percent for "all other" females, 27 percent of these women were reclassified during the follow-up period. The large proportion of those whose AFDC status was unaffected reflects the continued school attendance of their dependent children, with consequent retention of eligibility. (Federally reimbursable assistance ends when children reach the age of 21, regardless of school status.)

Closing rates are the inverse of those for continuous dependency, with males showing highest overall frequency—40 percent, rising to over 50 percent for the youngest age group. Although age affects the likelihood of termination differentially in the case of the three subpopulations, it is noteworthy that this difference disappears between females with older dependents and males 45 years and over, who show a common closing rate of 35 percent. Similarly there is no difference between female household heads with a single dependent aged 18 and all other female household heads in the 35–44 age bracket, a proportion of whom have fairly young children. Apparently, once children reach the age where they no longer require intensive personal care, their presence at home does not independently influence the mother's capacity for self-support.

It is tempting to distinguish among recipients whose cases have closed between those who subsequently returned to dependency and those who did not. Although the brevity of the follow-up period limits the generalizability of the comparisons, to the extent that reopenings following closings within the H-DRAT period may be considered representative of brief welfare terminations generally it is noteworthy that these are very short-term interludes of self-sufficiency: overall, 70 percent reopened within six months of closing, and an additional 26 percent reopened in under one year. Males experienced significantly higher early-reopening frequency than household heads in either of the female categories (table 6.1). This would imply greater short-run mobility by males and, in the case of this sample, administrative efforts during the period of the H-DRAT follow-up to impel male recipients off the public assistance rolls, efforts which were thwarted in part by the limited resources available to these men to maintain self-support and by continuing high unemployment.

Of the one-third of the AFDC mothers with youngest dependent child aged 18 whose cases closed during the H-DRAT period, 25 percent were soon reopened—a lower rate than that of either the other females or the males. This number is, however, offset by the heavy flow of terminating AFDC recipients into other assistance categories.

Are there critical points in the welfare episode relevant to the likelihood of closure? Examination of the duration of dependency prior to closing indicates inverse trends between male and female populations, with male closing frequencies highest following one to two years of dependency (27 percent) and decreasing with lengthening dependency, as opposed to females, where the largest proportion in both sample categories are chronic dependents (56 percent for women whose youngest dependent child is nearing the age of 18, and 34 percent for all other women). It is of interest to note that by far the smallest number of case closings for both sexes were short-term cases, that is, under one year. Even among males who during this period were targeted for intensive termination efforts, closures were as low as 10 percent, reflecting the bleak employment prospects of even the presumably more employable within this group.

Turning directly to the reasons for assistance termination, one can see the limited, if ambiguous, role of job-related causation, a category which covers primarily employment but also includes increased earnings and in a very few cases receipt of unemployment-insurance benefits (table 6.2). By far the largest proportion of closings applicable to all three subpopulations are referable to administrative action ("refused compliance"). Consistent with the distribution of acceptance reasons (table 3.3), where unemployment resulting from health impairment or job loss was considerably more frequent among males than females, termination for job-related reasons applies more characteristically to males. Although almost 20 percent of case closings among AFDC mothers with a single 18-year-old dependent are for job-related reasons, this is true of a bare 10 percent of other females. Most conspicuous is the

Table 6.2 Reasons for First Closing in Follow-up Period January 1972–May 1973, by Sex and Age of Household Head (in percent)

Reason for first closing	Males				Females with youngest dependent child aged 18				All other females			
	18–24	25–34	35–44	Over 44	18–24	25–34	35–44	Over 44	18–24	25–34	35–44	Over 44
	(42)	(67)	(48)	(53)	—	(4)	(28)	(57)	(43)	(54)	(58)	(58)
Job-related	31	30	19	25	—	75	21	12	16	6	9	9
Non-job related	2	—	—	6	—	—	14	2	5	7	3	3
Decreased need	—	3	10	6	—	—	—	7	—	11	9	10
Refused compliance	36	39	44	28	—	25	32	42	28	26	41	43
Client's request	14	8	6	6	—	—	18	12	14	13	9	9
Miscellaneous	17	21	21	30	—	—	14	25	37	37	29	16

NOTE: Figures in parentheses represent absolute numbers.

disparity in frequency between job loss as a precipitant of welfare and explicit job return as a cause of welfare termination; this is true even if one discounts unemployment for reasons of health. The younger age groups are selectively the most likely to return to employment. If it is assumed that terminations due to client's request, miscellaneous (which includes subsequent disproval of eligibility and moving), and compliance refusal frequently result from the fact that jobs or other sources of income were found or that the client had had ongoing concealed employment, return to self-sufficiency via earnings becomes more significant; nonetheless, it does not correspond to the incidence of unemployment as an opening reason, and one cannot infer substantially greater work-welfare mobility. This finding is reinforced by analysis of second and third terminations on the H-DRAT file, representing 29 percent and 10 percent, respectively, of all who underwent any change in welfare status during this period, where compliance refusal rises to over 50 percent and job-related reasons decline to 11 percent for all age groups. The high percentage of administrative closings may reflect newly introduced requirements for face-to-face recertification and employables reporting to the state Employment Service during this period.

Short-Term Reopenings: The Outcome of
Welfare Termination from January to May 1972

The subset of recipients who left the welfare rolls during the first five months of the H-DRAT file closely resemble the total H-DRAT sample in demographic characteristics and accordingly justify further analysis that might differentiate between individuals who are able to maintain self-support and others who return promptly to public assistance. Restriction of this examination to cases terminated during the initial H-DRAT period yielded a follow-up interval ranging from one year to sixteen months. Since 40 percent of intervals bertween public assistance episodes for the entire sample averaged less than twelve months and an additional 13 percent reopened after an interval of one to two years, seventeen months was considered an adequate period for assessing return to dependency.

If one examines this subset of recipients whose cases terminated

69

in early 1972, younger males, aged 18 to 24, are consistently overrepresented, and older males, aged 35 and over, are under-represented. Although the absolute number of those who returned to the welfare rolls within a year is small, they constitute 29 percent of males and are even more heavily concentrated in the younger half of the age distribution (under 35 years). Not unexpectedly, the reverse pattern is true for female household heads, the more elderly of whom leave the welfare rolls for some period. Overall, fewer females (21 percent) than males returned to public assistance within a year of closing.

In comparing duration of assistance for the subset that closed during the first five months of 1972 with the entire DRAT sample, it should be recalled that later closure of the vast majority of the latter automatically lengthens duration findings. Nonetheless, the striking proportion (45 percent) of male early DRAT closures following 12 to 24 months of assistance suggests selective termination of more recently accepted recipients as the result of case review and the referral of all employable recipients to the Employment Service.

Consistent with the findings for all DRAT closures, explicit employment accounted for only a small proportion of terminations for both male and female recipients during the first half of 1972. Moreover, of the 20 percent of males whose earnings lifted them out of dependency, one in three returned fairly soon to welfare. Among females, employment effected termination for slightly over 10 percent of the cases, but these appear to be longer-lasting. The large percentage of closures subsumed under the category "client's request," particularly for males, suggests employment-generated income as well; if this is true, fully 35 percent of these male closures could be considered employment-related and may reflect the more stringent administrative policies of the period. Termination at the "client's request" suggests longer-term independence among men. Since employment is the reason for welfare termination among females less frequently than it is for males and "client's request" is less likely to reflect employment in the case of women, one may infer that work is not the most significant factor for the achievement or maintenance of self-support among women approaching middle age.

Summary

Interpretation of the work-welfare mobility data for the sample during the follow-up period is complicated by the continuation of the recession. The high unemployment rates in New York City during 1970 (4.8 percent) and 1971 (6.7 percent), the period when over 25 percent of the entire sample and 40 percent of all males were initially accepted for public assistance, increased to 7 percent in 1972. Accordingly, it may seem surprising that as many as 32 percent of all recipients were able to leave the welfare rolls. At the same time, there were vigorous efforts to eliminate employables from the caseload, primarily by the mandatory registration of able-bodied HR recipients with the Employment Service and secondarily through the WIN II (Talmadge Amendment) program. Changes in welfare status must be seen in the light of these countervailing forces.

Termination of assistance was heavily concentrated among younger males, although these episodes of independence were frequently short-lived. Among males, the likelihood of termination was greatest following one to two years of dependency, decreasing with time, while for females termination was more characteristic of longer-term recipients. The high rate of short-run terminations among males may be attributed in part to the work-oriented policy of the administration during the period, despite unfavorable economic conditions. Explicitly employment-related terminations were also highest for younger males (aged 18 to 34).

Relatively few AFDC mothers whose youngest child was aged 18 achieved any but brief independence; the great majority persisted as dependents either through recategorization or through retention of eligibility by virtue of the child's continued school attendance.

7

Summary and Conclusions

The distinction made by the Social Security Act between those who can support themselves and those who cannot is not based upon actual labor market operations. For work and welfare are closely intertwined. . . . The decision to accept welfare neither precludes participation in the labor force nor necessitates a long duration on public assistance.[1]

This view of a close nexus between work and welfare and its corollary, a dynamic rather than a static caseload, has gained wide currency over the last decade. Since 1967 this view has informed all major federal efforts at welfare reform seeking to stimulate work by welfare recipients through economic incentives combined with varying degrees of coercion.

This survey explored the work-welfare relationships of a sample of public assistance recipients. The locus is New York City, whose concentration of welfare beneficiaries is among the highest in the nation. The scale of New York's economy and of the heterogeneity of its population are atypical, and these and other unique characteristics suggest caution in generalizing from the findings. But New York also shares many characteristics with other large urban centers, and to this extent the findings are generalizable.

The population studied was selected to represent, not the total public assistance population, but only the most employable subgroups. The aged and disabled were excluded; male-headed families and female-headed families with a youngest child aged 18 were oversampled. By studying these groups we hoped to learn more about the nature of the work-welfare relationship.

Limited Work-Welfare Mobility

A typology of work-welfare mobility would have to include (a) one-time recipients of public assistance whose lifetime is otherwise characterized by continuous self-support, (b) intermittent beneficiaries who alternate between work and welfare, and (c) long-term recipients of assistance. The first are not identifiable in this inquiry, which surveyed current (1971) recipients and thereby eliminated cases closed after a single episode. However, the substantial number of persons receiving assistance for the first time during the recession years of 1970 and 1971 suggests that this group may constitute a subset of uncertain size and of distinct importance to the subject of study.

More amenable to analysis is intermittency, which may be estimated from the number of past dependency episodes and the reasons for acceptance and termination. Previous studies using aggregate statistics have estimated a high incidence of intermittent dependency. However, our data do not confirm much significant intermittency: while 30 percent of the sample have had multiple episodes of public assistance, only 10 percent have had three or more. Moreover, what causal evidence there is pertaining to intermittency reflects nonwork factors rather than seasonal or unstable employment.

Not surprisingly, adult males experience intermittent work and welfare more frequently than females. Although there is no variation in the number of welfare episodes by sex, the shorter total time on public assistance experienced by men argues for greater intermittency. However, even for men intermittency is minimal; viewed within the framework of the total caseload, only 5 percent of the males experienced at least two welfare episodes consequent to job loss. Among women the work-welfare connection is even looser. Since 1967, job loss has accounted for only one-fifth of all initial acceptances to the welfare rolls among females. Overall only an extremely small fraction of all female recipients have alternated between work and public assistance.

A further attempt to estimate work-welfare mobility was made through a follow-up of the initial 1971 sample in May 1973. Again greater mobility was found for the males, 40 percent of whom had left welfare, with one-third of this group returning before the end of the period. Among the women with a single dependent child aged 18 and "all other" women, one-third and one-quarter, respectively, left the welfare rolls, with a rate of return similar to that of the men. In each case the greatest mobility was found among the young.

Those who did leave the rolls during the follow-up period generally did not do so for job-related reasons. Among females less than 10 percent of the terminations were for job-related reasons, and the figure for males is about 25 percent. Terminations were most frequent among females receiving assistance for relatively long periods (five years or more), while males tended to close after durations of one to three years.

In general, findings of case closings due to employment must be accepted as minimal estimates. They represent only those persons who secured a job and promptly notified their caseworkers or were found by the caseworker to be working. Various administrative categories of termination reasons and "client's request" may be assumed to include an unknown number of already employed (licitly or illicitly) or newly employed recipients. In a period of vigorous departmental efforts to reduce the welfare rolls, a number of ineligibles must have been removed. Nevertheless, at a maximum, only a small proportion of the total caseload returned to self-sufficiency via employment earnings. While this finding may in part be explained by the poor economic conditions during the follow-up period, they are consistent with the pre-1971 evidence.

Marginal Labor-Force Attachment

Information on the previous work history of the sample indicates that, for many, attachment to the labor force was limited and peripheral. Over 68 percent of all recipients not currently employed had a total of less than six months documented experience during the four years preceding the survey. These were preponderantly women—in fact, nearly 80 percent of all nonworking women were in this category, but more than 25 percent of all the men also had less than six months of work experience in this period. At the time of the sample selection 58 percent of the men, but only about 15 percent of the women, were reported to be either working or looking for work. These figures obscure the fact that work among public assistance recipients is underreported, although the actual extent of such employment is indeterminate.

Age is the major determinant for the work status of men but not for that of women, for whom ethnicity is the crucial factor. A disproportionate share of men neither working nor looking for work are over the age of 45. The nonparticipation of older men is due of course to multiple causes, including discouragement and the presence of problems of various kinds. The reported incidence of health impairment was highest, for example, for those members of the sample neither working nor looking for work, and this differential was particularly striking among men.

Blue-collar jobs in manufacturing and a variety of unskilled jobs provided the major source of employment for those who had worked. For women, particularly black women, however, a shift to white-collar employment, reflecting the general trend in the New York City economy, is evident, and these white-collar jobs provided the highest wages for women. A wage differential favoring men persisted throughout; overall, however, the earnings of those who had worked were low for men and women alike. Even for those whose last job was in 1970–71, 45 percent of the men and 83 percent of the women earned less than $100 ($80 weekly in constant 1967 dollars). The rapid rise in welfare allowances beginning in 1966 made the incomes unskilled women could derive from the labor market increasingly unattractive. Under these circumstances, it is not unlikely that the low levels of employment reported for AFDC mothers reflect their conscious choice of welfare over available work.

The Currently Employed

Ten percent of the total sample is currently employed and constitutes a distinct subset. They are primarily males and heads of intact households. Despite limited schooling, they have stable jobs with service or manufacturing firms and have accumulated far greater work experience than other welfare recipients. Notwithstanding their stable work histories, the currently employed generally required public assistance supplementation because the size of their families made their pay levels inadequate even by minimal welfare standards.

75

Youthfulness of Recent Accessions

The youngest age group is conspicuous by its heavy representation among the most recent accessions to the welfare rolls and by its paucity of work experience. Overall, thirty percent of those who came on the rolls in 1970–71 are under 25—this age bracket constitutes the largest number of women and the second largest number of men. While it can be assumed that the recession of 1970–71 exacerbated to some extent the normal high youth unemployment rate, it is not clear whether this phenomenon is not also reinforcing a secular shift in the age composition of the welfare caseload.

Migrancy and Dependency

Migrancy, defined in this study as relocation from a birthplace outside New York State, is strikingly associated with dependency in New York City. Eighty percent of the total sample (predominantly blacks and Puerto Ricans) are of non–New York origin, a figure proportionate to the incidence of migrancy in the general population even when standardized for ethnicity. The vast majority of migrants, 85 percent, arrived after the age of 18. For migrant welfare household heads, the median pre-acceptance residency period in New York was three years, which suggests a failed attempt at self-maintenance rather than in-migration for the purpose of gaining prompt access to the state's liberal welfare system. Migrants are characterized by meager educational levels, often acquired in the rural South or Puerto Rico and generally inadequate for effective competition in the New York labor market. Moreover, cultural patterns influence work participation, as in the low employment rates of Puerto Rican women.

In sum, there is no singular welfare population, but a number of subpopulations differentiated by demographic characteristics and employability. For other than a small group of currently employed, the case record data reveal, however, that the gap between work and welfare is wide. The overwhelming majority of recipients are migrants who came to the city as adults and struggled for several years to achieve self-support. Most turned to welfare because of ill health or other non-job-related problems, and once they began to receive assistance, few were able to leave the rolls because they had found employment. Intermittent reliance on public assistance between periods of employment was rare; less than 5 percent of the males and even fewer females fell into this pattern.

Policy Implications

The study's findings indicate that current programs and economic conditions, at least in New York City, have not produced a common pattern of combined or alternating work and welfare incomes. New approaches taking account of differing degrees of employability are evidently required to increase the earned income of persons now dependent upon public assistance.

The goals of any new efforts should be set realistically. Self-support must be distinguished from work, even full-time work. While for many employment can be equated with self-support, for others work will not do away with the need for some transfer income. It is possible to consider measures which will maximize work effort but not necessarily eliminate dependency. Recommendations intended to promote this goal may be divided into two groups: (1) policies with a broad economic impact that affect welfare recipients as a part of the total population and (2) policies directed specifically at the income-transfer system.

The viability of a political decision that all adults except the severely disabled are responsible for generating some earned income depends upon the availability of an adequate supply of jobs. A soft labor market turns away the most ardent devotion to the work ethic and is hardly the instrument for the absorption of workers with limited skills and erratic work histories.

High employment levels or "full employment" is generally sought through national fiscal and monetary measures. No review is necessary here of the abundant literature devoted to mechanisms for shifting the Phillips curve to the left so that the combination of high levels of inflation and unemployment can be avoided. It seems obvious that whatever the route, a high rate of employment growth is a necessary if not a sufficient condition for increased self-support among recipients. This is true at both the national and local levels. For New York City, unless the decline in employment that has continued since 1970 is reversed, prospects for more work and less welfare are dim.

77

Even under conditions of full employment there are firms, usually small and labor-intensive and operating in competitive product markets, that pay wage rates so low that workers' incomes fall below welfare-eligibility levels. To put a floor under such wage rates and thus prevent the slide into welfare, legislation raising the minimum wage is sometimes suggested. While the wage effects of minimum-wage laws are obvious, their employment effects have for two decades been the subject of intense controversy. The advantages of higher wage rates must be weighed against the loss of employment opportunities for secondary earners, particularly youth. The general employment and inflationary consequences of raising minimum-wage levels to a point where the income from 35 to 40 hours of work would satisfy budgetary requirements at the lower level of living, as defined by the Bureau of Labor Statistics for a family of four, would probably make such a measure inadvisable. Finally, for the small group of working recipients who require supplementary assistance because of the large size of their families, an increase in the minimum wage alone would not bring their incomes above welfare-eligibility levels.

To date there has been no political consensus in favor of national policy that would guarantee employment to able-bodied individuals and also provide work for diverse categories of the hard-to-employ. Instead, government efforts to direct the poor to self-support have taken the form of changes in the public assistance system and of the development of supply-oriented programs.

With the heightened consciousness in the mid-sixties of the problem of poverty and the concern with the perverse growth of the welfare program during a period of prosperity, it became apparent that the welfare system had failed to provide adequately or equitably for the poor and that at the same time it contained intrinsic disincentives to work. That AFDC was no longer exclusively a program for unemployables was made explicit by the extension of eligibility to families with an unemployed parent, in addition to those with the traditional absent parent. The intensive social-services programs instituted in the early sixties for the rehabilitation of families had the implicit goal of ultimate self-support. But a strategy designed expressly to return welfare recipients to the labor market was first introduced in 1967 with the inclusion of the WIN program in the Social Security Amendments. Economic incentives to seek employment and training leading to employment—an income strategy rather than a services strategy —were introduced and have remained an essential element in the effort to reduce poverty via public assistance.

Public debate concerning welfare reform has pursued multiple objectives, in some respects overlapping but ultimately posing a dilemma whose resolution involves inevitable trade-offs. As currently perceived, a reformed welfare system, including one modeled on a negative income tax, must establish an adequate income floor for all, treat different family constellations equitably, and provide incentives to work—all within an acceptable total cost. The fatal flaw has been the inability to reach any political consensus on specific criteria to satisfy these objectives. The achievement of a workable formula is more than a technical problem: it involves priorities and judgments regarding employability and earnings potential. A basic grant level sufficient to relieve poverty, as it is commonly defined, coupled with earnings retention sufficient to induce work would involve a massive redistributive commitment currently beyond public acceptance. A high national grant level with a high earnings tax rate relieves poverty at the expense of work effort; a lower basic level with higher earnings retention penalizes the unemployable. The choice of alternatives should be guided by a realistic assessment of the employment potential of the beneficiary population.

Since it is clear that employability varies, perhaps different mixes of benefit level and work incentive would more equitably meet differential expectations while still maintaining the advantages of wage income for all. Differential treatment of dependent groups based on potential employability is already characteristic of U.S. income-transfer programs. The aged and disabled are subject to benefit and earnings-disregard provisions in the federal SSI program which differ from those available under the AFDC programs. AFDC, in turn, has more favorable work-incentive provisions than state general assistance programs. The basic issue is how to define different categories of employability.

Who among the able-bodied is employable? With the increasing voluntary participation of women with children of various ages in the labor force,[2] the original blanket Social Security definition of mothers with dependent children as unemployable is no longer tenable. Should differing female-headed family constellations be treated differentially? This has been the basic provision in WIN and the Talmadge Amendments, which have excepted mothers of young children from enrollment. Should age be another factor, and if so, what should be the cutoff age? Should prior work experience be a factor? And should there be any minimal level of skill and literacy? Is coercion to be adopted, or is a willingness to work essential to the definition of employables?

With the provision of sufficient support services and societal acceptance of coercion, all able-bodied recipients, regardless of age, experience, or skill, can be defined to be "employable." A 1972 study of the welfare caseload in New York City,[3] defining as employable all individuals aged 18 to 64 who are employed or who declare their availability for employment, found a total of 20 percent, ranging from 11.5 percent of AFDC to 40 percent of AFDC-U and 49 percent of HR. But with the provision of moderate assistance for child care and specific health and rehabilitative services to remove existing problems, an additional 30 percent, heavily concentrated in the AFDC caseload, are considered potentially employable.

Employability, however, is more than a sociological construct; in a realistic sense it is defined by economic considerations, specifically the state of the local economy. The supply of and the demand for workers with specific skills and experience are critical determinants. In an increasingly highly skilled service economy such as New York's, it seems clear that there will be insufficient jobs in the private sector permitting self-support for the large numbers of unskilled and poorly educated adult welfare recipients with marginal work experience that have emerged from our analysis. It would therefore seem preferable to identify specific target populations for the intensive services and economic incentives that would help integrate them into sectors of growing employment. Chief among these would be (1) adolescents in welfare families and young childless adults; (2) women in the prime working ages with recent work experience; and (3) prime-age men with recent work experience.

Adolescents in welfare families and young childless adults. For the younger age groups, who constitute the largest proportion of new accessions to the welfare caseload, the challenge is to establish early a lifetime pattern of self-support. The current dysfunction for many youths of the local high-school education is reflected in their high unemployment rate even in times of economic expansion. There is a need to forge stronger links between schools and employers to prevent the mismatch between skills and employment requirements that characterizes many of the older members of welfare families. The growth in New York City in the 1960s of industries and occupations requiring relatively high levels of literacy and new skills, coupled with the simultaneous decline in the manufacturing sector, the traditional employer of the unskilled, put additional demands upon the educational system. Neither educational leaders nor government officials have been unaware of the need for improved planning for occupational training to link it more directly to local labor-market requirements.[4] Employer-sponsored training, joint union-management apprenticeships, and career-oriented curricula in the community colleges are all features of the New York scene that deserve to be encouraged. Attention must be concentrated, however, on the large number of young people—an estimated 40 percent—who drop out of high school after tenth grade. While some make their own way into the labor market, others do not, and these receive insufficient attention from guidance and employment counselors. They should become the object of vigorous efforts to advise them of alternative school programs, out-of-school training programs, and the opportunity either to return to school or to obtain high-school-equivalency diplomas.[5]

Women in the prime working ages with recent work experience. By virtue of their age, experience, and higher educational levels, these women are "employable." However, most women in this category are receiving assistance because of childcare responsibilities, and the presence of young children often makes them unemployable by some definitions. Important questions arise as to the cost-benefit trade-off of daycare services and their generalized use, since the increase in the number of female-headed families in the general population and the increasing labor-force participation of mothers of young children pose the problem of providing adequate childcare services both for mothers currently working and for welfare mothers who seek work. At present, most children of working mothers do not make use of formal institutional day care; a variety of other much less expensive arrangements are made, involving primarily older nonemployed relatives, neighbors, and friends. But with the increasing rates of labor-force participation among younger women, attrition of these alternate sources of care may be anticipated. Against this, the decreasing birth rate among the welfare population should be noted in the formulation of long-term plans for childcare facilities. The money cost of publicly funded and operated daycare centers for all mothers or even for welfare mothers alone is high, and taxpayers should not expect any immediate reduction in the onerousness of their burden. In fact, the (present) cost of day care must be balanced against the (future) benefits accruing from the economic independence of the mother and the possible benefits to the child. Five years of daycare costs must be weighed against twenty to thirty years of dependency.[6] The attempt to provide a general system of day care under conditions of fiscal stringency has led to the imposition of eligibility and fee-scale requirements and has raised the problem of equity in the provision of such services. It does not seem unreasonable to make the expensive but ultimately sound investment in day care for younger children and more extensive kindergartens and after-school care for their older siblings a universally available component of the general school system.

Prime-age men (25 to 44 years) with recent work experience. This group, considered highly employable by most criteria, are now subject to the least favorable treatment with respect to economic work incentives. While female family heads benefit from a modest earnings disregard ($30 per month plus one-third of additional earnings) under the WIN amendments, working males in the state's Home Relief program do not have even this incentive. Extending equivalent work incentives to males would add to the state's fiscal burden by increasing grants for the currently employed but might reduce expenditures required for nonworking males. The available but low-paying jobs listed at state Employment Service offices might be more readily accepted if employable males were provided some economic incentive for taking such jobs. While continued supplementation to low-wage jobs is a likely prospect for many male recipients, some may be able to attain complete self-support. For those whose employment was terminated by the recession of 1970 (20 percent of all men in the sample) an upturn in the economy may be sufficient to return them to self-support. This would seem most likely in the case of those who lost white-collar jobs or skilled blue-collar jobs in the more viable sectors of the economy. On the other hand, many will have fewer opportunities for reemployment; their scanty education and lack of skills have been reported to be the most important single obstacle to placement and indicate the need for (re)training for specific blue-collar and service occupations.[7] Manpower programs directed at improving the employability of adults have had mixed results at both the national level and within New York City. But the *sine qua non* for success in all cases has been direct linkage to employers with available jobs. From the accumulated experience of WIN and MDTA, the preferred approach to retraining seems to be OJT, since it offers the best opportunity for job retention and advancement.

The combination of work incentives and services described above would enable and encourage many of those now receiving assistance to increase their work effort. However, many others will remain totally dependent. For this group of men and women past their prime working years who have been separated from the labor market for several years or who have had no work experience at all and frequently have physical and emotional health problems, and for others whose marginal stability precludes effective functioning in the normal workplace, self-support does not seem an appropriate goal. Included here would be the large majority of AFDC mothers with a single dependent child approaching the age of 18. In fact, the issue is whether even an expanded work effort should be assigned priority. Even under conditions of rapid economic growth, this group could probably secure employment only in a sheltered environment. Although there is little American experience with such programs, western European models indicate that the cost of government acting as an employer of last resort is greater than that of direct income maintenance. This cost would be justified only in terms of a social commitment to provide employment for all who want to work. While this is certainly a desirable benefit, it must be realized that it is not a measure which can yield savings to the taxpayer.

In the middle ground between those who with sufficient training can make their way unaided in the labor market and those who can only operate, if at all, within a protected setting are the unskilled and semi-skilled, for whom only the presence of a secondary worker can permit a decent standard of living without recourse to public assistance supplementation. Although the sample data revealed the presence of only a small number of multiple-worker families, contrary to the trend in the general population, measures such as tax incentives and enhanced Social Security benefits might be adopted to stimulate work participation and strengthen family stability.

Finally, since migrancy is so closely related to dependency, particularly in New York City, a viable system of getting labor-market information to migrant populations seems warranted. Such a system was authorized by the 1968 amendments to the Manpower Development and Training Act to collect and publish information on job vacancies, to establish a computerized system of job matching and to expand Employment Service operations. Dissemination of accurate labor-market information in Employment Service offices in the South and in Puerto Rico might lead to the realization that although New York City is the place where friends and relatives have gone in the past, it is no longer the best place for those with few marketable skills and language barriers. Job-motivated migrants should be reoriented toward other parts of the country, such as the urban South and Southwest, where growth rates are higher and job opportunities are brighter.

Notes

CHAPTER 1

1. U.S. Department of Health, Education, and Welfare, Social Security Administration, *Social Security Bulletin*, Annual Statistical Supplement, 1972, table 138; U.S. Department of Commerce, *Statistical Abstract of the U.S., 1972*, table 37.

2. U.S. Department of Health, Education, and Welfare, Welfare Administration, Bureau of Family Services, Division of Program Statistics and Analysis, *Characteristics of Families Receiving Aid to Families with Dependent Children, November–December 1961*; U.S. Department of Health, Education, and Welfare, National Center for Social Statistics, *Findings of the 1967 AFDC Study: Part I, Demographic and Program Characteristics,* and *Findings of the 1969 AFDC Study: Part I, Demographic and Program Characteristics*; Elaine M. Burgess and Daniel O. Price, *An American Dependency Challenge* (American Public Welfare Association, 1963); U.S. Department of Health, Education, and Welfare, Social and Rehabilitation Service, *Reasons for Opening and Closing Public Assistance Cases*, NCSS Report A-5, 1969.

3. Gordon W. Blackwell and Rosmond F. Gould, *Future Citizens All* (American Public Welfare Association, 1952); Burgess and Price, *An American Dependency Challenge*; Lawrence Podell, "Mothers' Education and Employment," in *Families on Welfare in New York City*, mimeographed (New York: The Center for Social Research, Graduate Center, The City University of New York, 1967); Leonard H. Goodman, *Welfare Policy and Its Consequences for the Recipient Population: A Study of the AFDC Program* (U.S. Department of Health, Education, and Welfare, Social and Rehabilitation Service, Office of Research, Demonstration, and Training, 1969); Greenleigh Associates, *Public Welfare, Poverty Prevention or Perpetuation: A Study of the State of Washington* (New York, 1964).

4. U.S. Department of Labor, Bureau of Labor Statistics, Middle Atlantic

Regional Office, Regional Reports: No. 9, *Labor Experience of the Puerto Rican Worker;* No. 13, Urban Study Series, Poverty Area Profiles, *The Working Age Population–Initial Findings* (October 1969); No. 14, Urban Studies Series, Poverty Area Profiles, *Characteristics of the Unemployed* (May 1970); No. 19, Poverty Area Profiles, *The New York Puerto Rican: Patterns of Work Experience* (May 1971); No. 21, Poverty Area Profiles, *The Job Search of Ghetto Workers* (June 1971); No. 22, Poverty Area Profiles, *Working Age Non-Participants: Persons Not in the Labor Force and Their Employment Problems* (June 1971); No. 30, *Social, Economic and Labor Force Characteristics of Residents in New York City's Low Income Areas* (September 1972); and No. 34, *New York City in Transition: Population, Jobs, Prices and Pay in a Decade of Change* (July 1973). Also Joe A. Miller and Louis A. Ferman, *Welfare Careers and Low Wage Employment* (U.S. Department of Labor, Manpower Administration, December 1972); Edward M. Opton, Jr., *Factors Associated with Employment among Welfare Mothers* (Berkeley, Calif.: The Wright Institute, 1971).

5. Eli Ginzberg et al., *New York is Very Much Alive: A Manpower View* (New York: McGraw-Hill, 1973); Department of Labor, *New York City in Transition.*

6. New York City Manpower Area Planning Council, Human Resources Administration, *Comprehensive Manpower Plan, New York City Fiscal Year 1974*, vol. 1, p. 11.

7. U.S. Department of Commerce, *1970 Census of Population*, C-34, table 85.

8. By definition the labor force includes individuals seeking employment as well as the employed; hence some welfare recipients are included.

9. The labor market, in the conceptualization usually associated with Peter B. Doeringer and Michael J. Piore, is a dual market, divided into a primary and a secondary sector. The primary labor market, mainly restricted to white adult males by virtue of discriminatory entrance practices, is characterized by high wages, employment security, and opportunities for advancement, while the secondary labor market, in which minorities, women, and teenagers usually find employment, is associated with low wages, intermittent employment, and dead-end jobs. High welfare rates among urban minorities are explained by resistance to continued employment in the secondary sector (Peter B. Doeringer and Michael J. Piore, "Unemployment and the 'Dual Labor Market,' " *The Public Interest* 38 (Winter 1975): 67-79). For some of the difficulties of categorizing jobs according to these criteria, see Albert Rees, "Low-Wage Workers in Metropolitan Labor Markets," in *The Future of the Metropolis: People, Jobs, Income*, ed. Eli Ginzberg (Salt Lake City: Olympus Publishing Co., 1974); and Ruth F. Lowell, *The Dual Labor Market in New York City* (Working Note Presented at Human Resources Administration Welfare Research Conference, New York City, 1 December, 1973).

CHAPTER 2

1. Data on age at in-migration were available for 971 household heads in the sample. Of this group 151, or 16 percent, were under age 18 at the time of in-migration.

CHAPTER 3

1. City of New York, Human Resources Administration, Department of Social Services, *Monthly New York City Public Assistance Summary, 1960-1973*, May 1974.

2. Department of Health, Education, and Welfare, *Characteristics of Families Receiving Aid to Families with Dependent Children, November–December 1961; Findings of the 1967 AFDC Study: Part I; Findings of the 1971 AFDC Study, Part I: Demographic and Program Characteristics.*

3. Greenleigh Associates, *Public Welfare, Poverty Prevention or Perpetuation.*

4. "Characteristics of AFDC Families in New York State," New York State Department of Social Services, Program Analysis Report No. 44, May 1969; Department of Health, Education, and Welfare, *Characteristics of Families Receiving Aid to Families with Dependent Children, November–December 1961; Findings of the 1967 AFDC Study: Part I; Findings of the 1971 AFDC Study: Part I.*

5. C. Peter Rydell, et al., *Welfare Caseload Dynamics in New York City*, The New York City–Rand Institute and Office of Policy Research, Department of Social Services, Human Resources Administration, City of New York, November 1973.

6. Department of Health, Education, and Welfare, *Characteristics of Families Receiving Aid to Families with Dependent Children, November–December 1961; Findings of the 1967 AFDC Study: Part I; Findings of the 1971 AFDC Study: Part I.*

7. Irving Leveson, "The Effect of Abortion Reform on AFDC Caseloads," Office of Health Systems Planning, New York City Health Services Administration, June 1973.

8. The figures for those continuously in assistance in table 3.4 differ from the two figures for those with one acceptance in table 3.1 because of differing response rates to questions concerning number of acceptances and those concerning acceptance reasons. Response was lower for acceptance reasons, and the bias in nonresponse raises the proportion reported as interrupted in table 3.4.

CHAPTER 4

1. U.S. Department of Commerce, Bureau of the Census, *New York: Detailed Characteristics*, PC (1)-D34, table 176 (1970). Figures are for the New York SMSA.

2. U.S. Congress, Subcommittee on Fiscal Policy, Joint Economic Committee, *Income-Tested Social Benefits in New York: Adequacy, Incentives, and Equity*, prepared by Blanche Bernstein, Studies in Public Welfare, no. 8, Washington 1973, table 3, supplement III.

3. Labor-force participation rates are lower for Puerto Rican (and Mexican-American) women (but not for Cuban women) than for black or white women (*Manpower Report of the President*, March 1973, pp. 97-98).

4. Given the limited period of 46 months, the requirement of a 3-month minimum work duration used to define an "effective" work history was dropped.

CHAPTER 5

1. Since the focus is on the *job* rather than the jobholder, jobs of less than three months duration are included. On this basis, a total of 1,724 jobs were identified. Of these, 153 were jobs held by those currently employed, and 1,571 were terminated jobs. However, occupation-industry data were reported for only 752 terminated jobs and 138 current jobs. This smaller data base is analyzed in this chapter.

2. Ginzberg et al., *New York is Very Much Alive*, chaps. 2, 4, 5, 6, and 7; U.S. Department of Labor, Bureau of Labor Statistics, Middle Atlantic Regional Office, *Some Facts Relevant to the Current Social and Economic Scene in New York*, March 1973; and *New York City in Transition*, p. 18.

3. Department of Labor, *New York City in Transition*, p. 18.

4. Department of Labor, *Some Facts Relevant to the Current Social and Economic Scene in New York*, p. 14.

5. Department of Labor, *New York City in Transition*, p. 4.

6. Introduction of the ethnicity variable reduces the job data base by somewhat over 10 percent because of lack of data on the ethnicity of the jobholder.

7. Data were available only for cash wages. In-kind payment, such as free rent for building superintendents and free food for restaurant, hotel, and domestic workers, is not included. In addition, it must be emphasized that wages are weekly wages and include weekly earnings of part-time employees.

8. In mid-1974 a (1967 constant dollar) wage of $80 equals approximately $123 in current dollars.

CHAPTER 6

1. Although the DRAT file commenced 1 January 1972, leaving a data gap for the period November–December 1971, immediately following the completion of the questionnaires, it was possible through examination of initial entries to detect the likely occurrence of activity during these two months. Thus a first H-DRAT entry for a specific case which was an opening or reopening, rather than the more usual closing, implied that the case had closed in the interval, and it was treated as such. Some significant information may have been lost regarding an unknown number of cases which closed in this period and did not reopen and whose consequent absence from the H-DRAT data was erroneously interpreted as uninterrupted dependency. A maximum number of such cases based on H-DRAT data for succeeding months would account for an error of 2.5 percent to 3 percent.

CHAPTER 7

1. Sar A. Levitan, Martin Rein, David Marwick, *Work and Welfare Go Together*, Policy Studies in Employment and Welfare no. 13 (Baltimore: Johns Hopkins Press, 1972), p. 49.

2. "The steepest rise in work propensity has been among women with children under 3, whose labor force participation rate increased by three-quarters, from 15.3 percent in 1960 to 26.9 percent in 1972" (*Manpower Report of the President*, March 1973, p. 66).

3. David L. Lyon, *The Employable Welfare Poor in New York City and Their Search for a Job*, AWN-8184-NYC (New York: The New York City–Rand Institute, 1973).

4. Eli Ginzberg, *Career Guidance: Who Needs It, Who Provides It, Who Can Improve It* (New York: McGraw-Hill, 1971).

5. David Lewin, et al., *The Urban Labor Market: Institutions, Information and Linkages* (New York: Praeger, 1974), chap. 5.

6. Ralph D. Husby, "Day Care for Families on Public Assistance: Workfare versus Welfare," *Industrial and Labor Relations Review*, July 1974, p. 510.

7. Blanche Bernstein, Michael Rowan, and Anne N. Shkuda, *Obstacles to Employment of Employable Welfare Recipients*, (New York: Center for New York City Affairs, New School for Social Research, June 1974), pp. 82 ff.

Index

Library of Congress Cataloging in Publication Data

Ostow, Miriam.

Work and welfare in New York City.
(Policy studies in employment and welfare no.
21)
"Prepared for the Manpower Administration, U.S.
Department of Labor, under research contract 21–36–
73–51."
Includes bibliographical references and index.
1. New York (City)—Poor. 2. Public welfare—
New York (City) 3. Unemployed—New York (City)
I. Dutka, Anna B., joint author. II. United
States. Dept. of Labor. Manpower Administration.
III. Title.
HV4046.N6087   362.5   75–11357
ISBN 0–8018–1735–8
ISBN 0–8018–1736–6 pbk.